Erratum

P.17   4th paragraph: "Susan and Staite" should read "Susan Staite"

P.18   Last paragraph: "Appendix II" should read "Appendix III"

P.19   1st paragraph: "English definitions of mental handicap" should read "traditional English definitions of mental handicap"

P.32   4th paragraph: "Cri de Chat" should not be in italics

P.59   5th paragraph: third line should read: "taken over by the newly formed NHS in 1948 . . ."

P.69   Under Social work: "GMHT" should read "CMHT"

P.74   2nd paragraph: the full reference is R. Burns and S. Kaufman (1971) *Kinetic Family Drawings*, Constable

P.99   Comments on the Invalid Care Allowance should read: "for adults caring for a severely handicapped person. A decision pending in the European Court may enable married women to claim".

P.110   "Noral" should read "Norval"

P.114   The Down's Children's Association telephone number is 01-580 0511/2

P.121   "1914-1959" should read "1913-1959"

P.128   "Actiology" should read "Aetiology".

Mental Handicap

A practical guide for social workers

Peter Gilbert

Business Press International
1985

Published in 1985 by
Business Press International Ltd
Quadrant House, The Quadrant, Sutton, Surrey SM1 4QQ

© 1985 Peter Gilbert
ISBN 0617 00447-1

Set in 11/11 Baskerville Roman Medium and
printed in Great Britain by Geo. H. Hine & Co., London

To Sue,
and Mary, Joanna and Ruth

PETER GILBERT is social work team leader at the Forest Hospital, Horsham, West Sussex, and a founder member of the Mid-Downs community mental handicap team. Following five years in the army and a degree in modern history at Balliol College, Oxford, he joined West Sussex social services department in 1974 and took a master's degree in social work at Sussex University. Having worked as a general social worker with special interest in mental handicap, the author was appointed in 1981 to his present post which has a casework, teaching and developmental role.

Peter Gilbert is co-author of two information handbooks for parents and contributed the chapter on the role of the social worker for the 1985 successor to "Tredgold's" — *Mental Handicap: A Multi-Disciplinary Approach*, edited by Professor Joan Bicknell. He has also contributed to the forthcoming Lion publication *Social Work: A Christian perspective* (to be published in 1986), and is co-author with Dr Peter Dickens of a University of Sussex Monograph, *The State and the Housing Question*.

The author is involved in the multi-disciplinary approach in both direct work, development and teaching. He is a member of the specialist panel for the English National Board's post-qualifying course for nurses in the field of mental handicap and was one of the social work contributors for the ENB training pack for RNMH nurses, *Caring for People with Mental Handicap* (1985).

The author would like to acknowledge the help and encouragement he has received from Colin Brunt, Jim Weston, Barry Spooner, colleagues in health and social services in West Sussex and also the tutorial staff on the MSW course at Sussex University. Especial thanks to Benny Goodman for his help with chapter 13, and to Dr Sheila Hollins of St. George's Hospital, London and Terry Scragg of Bognor College for their advice on the content. Thanks are also due to Margaret Allott and Margaret Williams for their patience in typing the text.

Despite good advice there remain the inevitable simplifications of a basic handbook and any lack of justice done to particular sections is entirely the author's responsibility.

The author and publishers would like to thank the following for kind permission to reproduce their material in this book (numbers of the pages where this material occurs are given in brackets): Advisory Centre for Education (90–91); S. Hewitt and Allen & Unwin (47); Bailliere Tindall (12); British Institute for Mental Handicap (92); Her Majesty's Stationery Office (21, 22–23); MIND (85); NFER-Nelson (55); Routledge & Kegan Paul (45); Souvenir Press (89, 101); The Disablement Income Group (48–49); Mrs Margaret Walker on behalf of the Makaton Vocabulary Development Project (96).

All author's royalties from this publication have been donated to:
The Royal Society for Mentally Handicapped Children and Adults (MENCAP) and Court Meadow School Association, West Sussex.

9

Contents

Introduction

"**S**omeone being slow, they are way down low". These lines are the start of a poem written by Roger Meyers, a mentally handicapped man who fought the system to hold down a job, marry his girlfriend and gain a home of their own. Mentally handicapped people and their families are usually in the position of having to fight for their rights as they remain a low priority for public services.

It is generally acknowledged that, in the decade following Seebohm, field social work as a whole showed little interest in working with mentally handicapped people and their families. There are many reasons for this: the trauma of reorganisation and the consequent dilution of specialist skills; the child abuse scandals of the seventies; the feeling among social workers that mental handicap was an irremediable condition; and the belief that casework skills were neither relevant nor effective in this area of work, and that "practical solutions" were all that was needed.

Lately, however, a change of attitude has been apparent and social services departments are appointing staff to work in multi-disciplinary teams. In the meantime a lot of knowledge and expertise has been dissipated and many workers are uncertain of their role in relation to that of psychologists and community nurses.

I have planned this publication to include the kind of knowledge that I would have found useful to have in the first years after qualification and when I was starting to specialise. I hope that it will give both some basic information and some guidelines for more detailed reading to the generic social worker in a busy area or patch office; to the student grappling with tomes of complex information; to residential and day care staff working from a resource centre; and to the social worker about to move into multi-disciplinary team work.

Persons with a mental handicap have not only their own unique human value as individuals but are also a signpost in our search for a moral perspective in society. As one religious leader said at the time of the Falklands conflict, when there was such an emphasis on machismo: "Without the presence of these people in our midst we might be tempted to think of health, strength and power as the only important values to be pursued in life".

If this guide stimulates interest in this field of work and brings a conviction that social work has a vital role to play in the mental handicap services then it will have been worth writing.

Peter Gilbert
April 1985

1

Definitions of disability

Concepts

It is a measure of our own conditioning that, in an age when individual gifts are so highly prized, we still tend to treat mentally handicapped people as a homogeneous group. Likewise individual handicapped people are often spoken of as merely the sum of their disabilities. While we would never dream of referring to our next-door-neighbour as Joe with five GCEs, one still finds plenty of references in written records to "severely subnormal man who cannot wash or dress himself".

Mental handicap is not a single condition. Although specific syndromes have been identified, the variation in ability amongst those with any syndrome differs widely, and, in fact, most mental handicaps are undefined. Mental handicap is not a disease or illness, though it may be caused by one, and it should not be seen as a condition requiring primarily medical attention unless perhaps it is complicated by other factors such as severe epilepsy or mental illness.

Although the terms impairment, disability and handicap are now often used inter-changeably, the World Health Organisation has tried to define each term in such a way as to help us understand how society relates to disability.

Impairment is a physical, psychological or neurological disorder. It may be temporary or permanent and can be present at birth or acquired subsequently. It is useful to regard impairment as an objective description of the loss of function.

Disability is the outward experience of the intrinsic situation. It exists when the impairment creates restrictions on the performance of those functions and activities which are regarded as the basic elements of everyday living: mobility, communicating with others, self-care and independence skills, and a meaningful occupation.

Handicaps are disadvantages preventing the fulfilment of roles that are normal, relative to chronological and cultural factors. Handicap represents the profound effects of impairment and disability which affect the whole person, not just selective faculties.

Furthermore, the concept of handicap shows a complex inter-relation between the intrinsic impairment, the psychological makeup of the individual, the strengths and weaknesses of family and social networks, and society's attitudes. If the last three factors are not able to overcome the disadvantages of the first, then impairment and disability lead on to handicap. It may be true to say, therefore, that "disability" only becomes a "handicap" if the individual, or alternatively society, is unable to develop compensatory strategies. This is as true of the family with a handicapped member as it is for the individual. There is an aphorism, prevalent today, that "a handicapped child creates a handicapped family". This is by no means so, as many parents develop the strategies which enable the whole family to rise above the restrictions imposed by the limitations of one member.

Example I Thomas was an adolescent with Down's Syndrome (impairment) who had poor speech and a heart defect (disability). His parents were naturally reluctant to over-extend their son or to allow him an independence which might endanger his health. In middle age he was still living at home, with elderly parents and a shrinking circle of friends and opportunities (handicap).

Example II Jacob had been to a school for children with moderate learning difficulties (formerly known as ESN(M) — see appendix III) and held down a job until he was placed in a mental handicap hospital, on a court order, for a minor sexual offence. On discharge, Jacob found life outside the institution very demanding, but, with help from his social worker and community nurse, he resisted the temptation to opt for admission to a hostel and ATC. Jacob's success in gaining employment and a council flat, and his eventual marriage, was a de-handicapping experience.

Figure 1: *Concepts of Disability*

Disease or Disorder $\rightarrow$	Impairment $\rightarrow$	Disability $\rightarrow$	Handicap
$\downarrow$	$\downarrow$	$\downarrow$	$\downarrow$
Intrinsic situation	Experience recognised as functional limitation	Experience defined as activity restriction	Experience socialised as disadvantage

Example III Mr and Mrs Smith had a severely mentally handicapped daughter with an unspecified condition (impairment). The mutual guilt and poor support from relatives and statutory services, locked them into an isolated self-recriminatory relationship which further isolated their child (handicap).

A widely-used system of classifying disabilities was drawn up by Dr Agerholm in 1973, which gives a wider perspective to disability than by concentrating on specific clinical conditions:

☐ Motor — affecting mobility, posture, manipulation.
☐ Visceral — ingestion, excretion.
☐ Communicative — receptive, expressive.
☐ Intellectual — delay, retardation, memory impairment.

16

☐ Emotional — psychosis, behavioural disorders, drug addiction.
☐ Invisible — metabolic disorder, epilepsy etc.
☐ Visible — skin disorders, scar tissue.

Pupils in the special schools for children with severe learning difficulties (formerly ESN(S) schools), or ATCs/SECs (adult training centre/social education centre) might well have such an impairment as to produce disabilities in a number of the above categories. It would not be uncommon for a vaccine-damaged child, for example, to have a loss of mobility, which in turn affects visceral functioning, coupled with intellectual impairment and epilepsy.

Definitions of mental handicap

Throughout the decades, attempts have been made to define mental handicap in a variety of ways: medical, social, legal, functional and educational. Most of these definitions have been negative in describing individual capacity, for example, "severe subnormality means a state of arrested or incomplete development of mind which includes subnormality of intelligence and is of such a nature or degree that the patient is incapable of living an independent life or of guarding himself against serious exploitation" (Mental Health Act 1959)
or express fear:
"... those who from an early age displayed some permanent mental defect, coupled with strong vicious or criminal propensities, on which punishment had little or no effect" (definition of "moral defectives" in the Mental Deficiency Act 1913).

Some kind of categorisation is required for service planning and delivery to take place, and this has mainly been done through intelligence quotients.

Figure 2: *Calculating Intelligence Quotients*

$$\frac{\text{Mental Age}}{\text{Chronological age}} \times 100 = \text{I.Q.}$$

The danger is that this can lead to a rigidity of approach whereby individuals can be locked into a system which predicts their prognosis for the rest of their life. The unreliability of such prediction has been shown recently with some community housing projects, where a low IQ has clearly been no bar to coping in an independent living environment (see Susan and Staite and David Torpy, "Who Can Live Alone?", *Mental Handicap*, Vol. 11 No. 3, September, 1983).

The World Health Organisation recognises the following classifications of mental handicap:

● Mild mental handicap (IQ 52–67) may be only a matter of delayed development. Children can be educated and adults can work in ordinary employment following training. They may lead independent lives and never be classified as being mentally handicapped

- Moderate mental handicap (IQ 36–51). Affected people are obviously handicapped but may learn self-help skills and work in sheltered employment.
- Severe mental handicap (IQ 20–35). There may be delayed development or failure to develop physical and communication skills. Often, affected people are also physically handicapped but they can still show limited independence.
- Profound mental handicap (IQ 0–19). Affected people require 24 hour care. Physical and sensory development may be grossly impaired.

The English system has broader bands:

Figure 3: *The Stratification of IQ Levels (UK)*

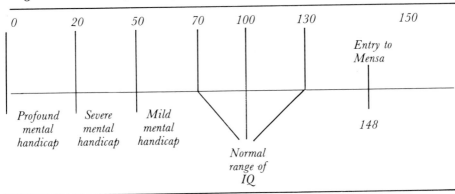

Although I have tended to use the most widely accepted phrase "mental handicap" throughout the text I have also used others such as "intellectual impairment" when it seemed right to distinguish between a clinical condition which impairs learning and functioning, as opposed to handicap which has as much to do with society's attitudes as the original clinical condition. It is confusing that the 1983 Mental Health Act uses the terms "mental impairment" and "severe mental impairment" to describe mentally handicapped people who may be dealt with under the same legislative sanctions as those suffering from a "mental illness" or "psychopathic disorder" (see below and chapter 13).

The development of terminology (see appendix II) has moved away from medical and legal parameters mainly towards concepts concerned with developmental and functional abilities. Since the passing of a consolidating Mental Health Act in England and Wales in 1983, mental handicap is no longer in itself legally defined. Mentally handicapped people have been largely taken out of mental health legislation unless, besides having "a severe impairment of intelligence and social functioning", they also show "abnormally aggressive or seriously irresponsible conduct". It should also be noted that English definitions of mental handicap require that the handicap occur before the achievement of full physical maturity. A 30 year old brain-injured in a car crash may function at a minimal level but is not technically mentally handicapped.

The 1981 Education Act, with its accent, albeit cautious, on integration, stemming from the Warnock report of 1978, is also likely to achieve a more positive outlook, concentrating on the talents of individuals not their deficits. This retreat from creating a "handicapped person" out of a sum total of functional disabilities will only be confirmed if society as a whole responds in a positive manner. As the American psychologist, Marc Gold, wrote: "Mental retardation refers to a level of functioning which requires from society significantly above average training procedures and superior assets in adaptive behaviour, manifested throughout life".

Our task as social workers is to look, see, think and speak positively and beat the predictions of pessimism.

Reading

D. Thomas (1982), *The Experience of Handicap*, Methuen.

M. Philip and D. Duckworth (1982), *Children with Disabilities and Their Families: A Review of Research*, Chapter 1, NFER-Nelson.

A. Shearer (1981), *Disability: Whose Handicap?* Blackwell.

P. Mittler (1979), *People, not Patients*, Chapter 2, Methuen.

D. Clarke (1982), *Mentally Handicapped People: Living and Learning*, Bailliere Tindall.

2
Numbers

J ust as with classification, estimates concerning the numbers of people with mental handicap in the United Kingdom need to be treated with extreme caution. Most of the figures currently quoted are derived from surveys carried out in Wessex, Newcastle and Camberwell and set out in the 1971 White Paper. Apart from the obvious fact that these areas may not be at all typical, there are considerable problems in identification and recording. For many young children with some degree of developmental delay it would be quite inappropriate to be labelled mentally handicapped, so that numbers are usually fluid until well into school age. In some authorities no register is kept at all. This raises the concepts of "true" prevalence — those who are within the below normal IQ range and "administrative" prevalence — those who receive some form of specialist service. The latter category is dependent, therefore, on service policy and delivery.

Table 1 *Causes of Severe Mental Handicap*

12%	—	Undefined condition
10%	—	Acquired (includes infections and irradiation)
10%	—	Ante-natal or perinatal injury
3%	—	Postnatal injury
2%	—	Child psychosis
43%	—	Genetic or chromosomal abnormalities
2%	—	Multiple congenital abnormality

Severe mental handicap

Recent estimates place the number of severely mentally handicapped people in Great Britain at about 160,000. This corresponds to a figure of four to five out of every 1000 children and two out of every 1,000 adults: a total of about 600 people in the average district health authority of 250,000.

Although better ante-natal care and screening techniques have lowered the chances of people having a mentally handicapped child, more multiply handicapped infants are surviving because of advances in medical technology. Technological medicine, however, is not in itself an unmixed blessing, as techniques developed in the seventies to keep small-for-dates

Table 2 *Changes Proposed in the 1971 White Paper and Progress Achieved*

Type of Provision	Number of places in England and Wales in 1969	Number of places proposed for 1991	Proposed increase/ decrease	Number achieved by 1977
Residential care in hospital (children).	7,400	6,400	– 1,000	3,900
Residential care in hospital (adults).	52,000	27,000	– 25,100	44,100
Residential care in the community (inc. short stay)				
(i) In local authority or privately owned residential homes				
Children	1,800	4,900	+ 3,100	2,200
Adults	4,300	29,400	+ 25,100	11,700
(ii) Foster homes, lodgings etc.				
Children	100	1,000	+ 900	not known
Adults	550	7,400	+ 6,850	739 (in 1975)
Occupation and training in the community for adults.				
(i) Living in the community	24,000	63,700	39,200	⎫
(ii) Coming by day from hospital	100	9,800	9,700˙	⎬ 38,700 ⎭

(Derived from DHSS, 1971 and DHSS, 1980)

babies alive in themselves caused functional disabilities while preserving life.

Although the incidence of severe mental handicap is fairly evenly spread across all social classes there is a higher risk to some cultural groups whose diet is unbalanced and hereditary conditions are not always picked up in deprived inner city areas where resources for screening are lacking.

Age is also a factor in handicap. There is a higher element of risk of having a Down's Syndrome child for mothers as they get older: 1:2000 at age 20; 1:100 at age 40; 1:46 at age 45. The survival rate amongst those with severe disabilities means that there will be a growing concentration of need in the older age brackets towards the turn of the century. With severe mental handicap it is much more likely that causal factors will be established than with mild mental handicap.

Mild mental handicap

Mild mental handicap has an incidence of about 15 out of every 1,000 of population and has a bias towards social classes IV and V. Social and cultural disadvantage are much more important factors here than "true" handicap and very few of those in schools for children with moderate learning difficulties would be classed as "mentally handicapped" by their teachers.

Demographic and social changes affect this group profoundly. For instance, the fall in birth rate and concern over school rolls has led to more children with learning difficulties being retained by their comprehensive schools rather than referred to "M" schools. On the other hand this de-handicapping factor is balanced by the number of "M" school leavers being forced by unemployment to seek places in adult training centres (A. Crine, "Two-way Squeeze", *Community Care*, 24 March, 1983).

Place of residence	Degree of mental handicap	Non-ambulant		Behaviour difficulties requiring constant supervision		Severely incontinent	
		0–14 years	15 + years	0–14 years	15 + years	0–14 years	15 + years
Home	Severe	10.49	3.18	4.83	3.17	5.00	1.69
Hospital or other residential care	Severe	6.10	7.23	4.86	15.58	3.65	6.97
	Mild	0.34	1.51	0.88	5.29	0.15	0.64
Total		16.81	11.92	10.27	24.01	8.75	9.30

Table 3   *Incapacity associated with mental handicap (rate per 100 000 total populat*

Figure 4   *Proportions of people with a mental handicap*

0	Profound	20	Severe	50	Mild	70
						IQ

5%		20%		75%	

Residential care

Surveys show that about 80 per cent of children with mental handicap and 40 per cent of severely mentally handicapped adults live at home. Significantly it is clear from the White Paper statistics and subsequent research that there is no easy correlation between the degree of handicap and admission to residential care. The White Paper (see Table 3) showed that out of every 100,000 population where there were six children in residential care who could not walk, there were 10 being cared for at home. While five children with severe incontinence were at home, only less than four were away. The numbers of those with severe behaviour difficulties were roughly comparable. Residential care is often sought only when parents' health breaks down.

There are about 40,000 people living in mental handicap hospitals in England and Wales, and although one-third of all NHS beds are in hospitals for the mentally disordered only 13 per cent of the NHS budget is spent on them. Average spending per bed in a London teaching hospital is £80 per patient per day, while the comparable figure for a mental handicap hospital is only £24.

Needing assistance to feed, wash or dress		No physical handicap or severe behaviour difficulties		Incapacity not assessed		Total	
0–14 years	15 + years	0–14 years	15 + years	0–14 years	15 + years	0–14 years	15 + years
15.90	9.29	12.79	53.90	0.73	0.94	49.24	71.65
3.63	16.58	1.69	49.36	0.10	0.94	19.96	96.19
0.23	1.96	3.85	42.40	0.21	0.15	5.55	53.17
19.68	27.82	17.04	146.46	1.04	3.03	72.90	221.00

m DHSS, 1971 and reprinted by permission of the Controller of Her Majesty's Stationery Office)

Despite the fact that residents in hospital score very low in assessments measuring socialisation and orientation, the DHSS's 1970 survey of mental handicap hospitals showed that 81 per cent of adults were fully ambulant; 74 per cent fully continent; 63 per cent required little or no help with feeding or washing or dressing; and 69 per cent were free of behaviour disorders. These are encouraging figures for those committed to moving people out of large hospitals, but the 1971 White Paper targets for community provision are nowhere near being met (see Table 2), and local authority hostels are still tending only to accept hospital residents from the higher ability levels.

Reading
P. Mittler (1979), *People, not Patients*, Methuen, Chapter 3.
DHSS (1971), *Better Services for the Mentally Handicapped*, CMND 4683, HMSO.
B. Kirman and J. Bicknell (1975), *Mental Handicap*, Churchill Livingstone.
M. Craft (ed.) (1979), *Tredgold's Mental Retardation*, Chapter 1, 12th Edition, Bailliere Tindall.
R. Hudson, "No Place Like Home", *Community Care*, 19 April, 1978.
DHSS (1980), *Mental Handicap: Progress, Problems and Priorities*.

3

Historical background

"Mentally handicapped people", writes Joanna Ryan, "are still as hidden from history as they are from real life. What history they do have is not so much theirs as the history of others acting either on their behalf, or against them".

Throughout history, societies have imposed on to mentally handicapped people images and roles which stem from the prevailing cultural milieu. Wolfensberger identified a number of these potent images leading up to the present day (see figure 5).

Ancient times

Perhaps because the numbers of mentally handicapped people were not seen as a threat to society as a whole or perhaps because eccentric behaviour was often regarded as a gift from the gods in the Judaeo-Hellenistic world (see Plato's *Phaedrus*), the handicapped and insane were usually treated with kindness, or at least left to their own devices, while their property was protected.

Christian writings, as exemplified by the 16th century Swiss physician, Paracelsus, carry on the theme of earlier times that "fools" might well be nearer to God than so-called "wise men". In England, Edward II's Act of Parliament, *De Praerogativa Regis*, distinguished between mental illness (lunatics) and mental handicap (idiots) and made provision for the protection of their property.

Popular beliefs in medieval Europe also helped in the main to protect handicapped people. Deformed or disabled infants were thought to be "changelings", the fairies having stolen the child away and put a changeling in its place. Parents treated the disabled child well so that the fairies would likewise care for the stolen child. This concept is still alive in a different form, many parents feeling that the handicapped child is not intrinsically theirs (because all animals, including human beings, need to identify with a recognised image in their offspring) and that the burden of care should be shared with society.

The Reformation

The philosophy of medieval and Renaissance Christendom, that mentally handicapped people were "infants of the good God", gave way to the harsh

Figure 5   *Historical Attitudes and Responses*

Images and attitudes	*Service Response*
(1) *Sub human*	
Lacks the emotional and physical needs of normal people. Primitive and unpredictable behaviour.	No rights. Mentally handicapped people are segregated and controlled.
(2) *Threat to society*	
A weak mind in a strong body with potential for unpredictable behaviour and procreation (see John Steinbeck's novel, *Of Mice and Men*)	Control and segregation leading to a denial of freedom and possibly destruction.
(3) *The eternal child*	
Catered for as children with no responsibilities but no rights either.	Stress on care but not development.
(4) *Scapegoat*	
Tolerated and cared for until society comes under pressure.	Segregated and perhaps killed at times of societal stress.
(5) *The uneconomic unit*	
A burden on society when economic pressures are high.	Segregation into units to fit economics of scale and exploitation.
(6) *Burden on charity*	
Judgement of weakness from a strong moralistic standpoint.	Basic needs are met in return for submission and gratitude.
(7) *Objects of pity*	
Suffering individuals of whom no demands should be made.	Paternalistic. Shelter against risk. Low expectations.
(8) *Sick person*	
Seen as sick and the passive recipient of medical care.	Hospital model of care with emphasis on diagnosis and prognosis. All matters come under the auspices of the medical practitioner.
(9) *Developing individual*	
An optimistic view of the individual who is seen as having the potential for growth.	Stress on individuality, dignity and personal responsibility.

moralistic climate of the "Protestant" or "bourgeois" ethic, with its accent on personal success as a sign of God's favour. The reformers fought against what they saw as "natural man" and strove to create "social conditions which discouraged idleness" (C. Hill (1972), *The World Turned Upside Down*, Temple Smith). Luther exemplified this approach, proclaiming that mentally handicapped persons were a mass of flesh with no soul. He advocated drowning them at birth (Martin Luther, *Table Talks*).

Reform and Reaction

The 18th century is often held up by modern New Right thinkers as the golden age when the family cared for its own. In fact evidence suggests that many mentally disordered people were boarded out or placed in private homes well away from their families. Jane Austen, the novelist, and her family represent the epitome of Georgian harmony, close-knit family ties and Christian compassion, but Miss Austen's biographer, David Cecil, tells us that she had a brother, George, who "does not come into this story; he was mentally defective and from an early age spent his life away from home".

It was in 19th century France and Switzerland that interest in the mentally handicapped and the possibilities of progress began with physicians and educationalists such as Jean-Marc Itard and Edouard Séguin. As the latter declared in 1846: "While waiting for medicine to cure idiots, I have undertaken to see that they participate in the benefits of education".

Asylums for the protection and education of "idiots" were started in England following the example of the Swiss Guggenbuhl. Without the notion of domiciliary help, the asylums were seen as places of harmony and order compared with the neglect of the family or private boarding places (see W. Parry-Jones (1972), *The Trade in Lunacy*, Routledge and Kegan Paul). This ideal is perhaps most clearly expressed in a report on the Highgate Asylum (founded in 1847) quoted in the *Edinburgh Review:*

"The first gathering of the idiotic family was a spectacle ... sufficiently discouraging to the most resolved ... some had defective sight; most had defective or no utterance; most were lame in limb or muscle; and all were of weak and perverted mind. Some had been spoiled, some neglected; some were sullen and perverse; and some unconscious and inert ... some, terrified at scorn and ill-treatment, hid themselves in a corner from the face of man, as from the face of an enemy ...

"... here is now order, obedience to authority, classification, improvement, and cheerful occupation. Every hour has its duty; and these duties are steadily fulfilled".

The Highgate Asylum was the first of a number of charitable hospitals along with Starcross Asylum, Exeter (1864) and the Northern Counties Asylum, Lancaster (1870). The first public venture was the Darenth Training School built by the metropolitan authorities in the 1870s.

In 1886 the Idiots Act was passed to consolidate some of these ventures but it gave little fresh impetus, and the 1890 Lunacy Act ignored the distinction between mental illness and mental handicap made by its predecessor.

Inevitably the fracturing of traditional society caused by the Industrial Revolution and the disillusionment when the high expectations aroused by the reformers failed to materialise caused a reaction. By 1881 only three per cent of the 29,000 mentally handicapped people in statutory residential care were in settings designed specifically for them; the rest were in asylums set up under the 1845 Lunatics Act or in workhouses.

The causes of reaction were:

☐ The industrialisation of the work process.

☐ The survival of more handicapped infants through environmental changes.

☐ The pressing need for the whole family to work, leaving no one at home to care for the disabled member.

☐ The increasing mobility of the family.

☐ The increasing identification of ''idiots'', leading to fear of a decline in national intelligence.

In 1855 the Highgate Asylum moved to Redhill where it became the Royal Earlswood — now a Victorian monolith of over 800 beds.

At the end of the 19th century social policy was going in several directions at once. A series of education acts included handicapped children in the new system of compulsory education for all; empowered authorities to set up special classes or schools for ''imbecile'' and ''feeble-minded'' children; and recognised their special needs by extending education to 16 years. This radical legislation was not matched until the Education Acts of 1970 and 1981 (implemented in 1971 and 1983, respectively).

At the same time, however, the National Association for the Care of the Feeble-Minded, was moving down a different road, setting up colonies for the ''permanent care of the feeble-minded''.

The 20th century

Dr Langdon Down's identification of ''mongolism'' (Down's Syndrome) in 1866 was seen as evidence of the appearance of alien cultural types in a national genetic degeneration. The eugenics movement grew so strong that while the Education Acts of the late 19th century placed mentally handicapped children within the educational system, the Radnor Commission of 1908 recommended segregation, and this view was to a great extent encapsulated in the form of the 1913 Mental Deficiency Act.

Despite the strong movement in this country for the complete segregation, especially of the moderately handicapped group who were seen as a threat to society, ''. . . the Act, by its careful division of the method of protection into statutory guardianship, institutional care, and licence from the institution, made it possible for many defectives to continue living in the community while still receiving a degree of care and control'' (Jones, 1972).

Between the two World Wars the number of institutions specifically for mentally handicapped people grew and those placed in them rose from 2,000 in 1914 to 50,000 in 1939. The logical consequence of eugenic theories was seen in Hitler's Germany when thousands of mentally handicapped people went to the gas chambers.

In 1948 the advent of the NHS saw mental handicap institutions or "colonies" pass to medical control, though a medical "cure" for mental handicap was no further advanced than when Séguin wrote about it in the middle of the previous century. In the case of children, the Curtis committee, which did so much to improve conditions for children in general, saw mentally handicapped children as a medical responsibility and so the system of institutionalising sometimes very young children, was continued and extended (see Shearer, 1980).

The Mental Health Acts and beyond

The 1959 Mental Health Act put a greater accent on community care, but it was the denunciation of the hospital system in the enquiries into Ely and Farleigh Hospitals in the late 1960s which created a demand for government action. It appeared to most observers that the government had not only failed to promote community care, but had not even ensured minimum standards within the hospital system.

Since 1971, mentally handicapped children have come back into the mainstream of education after a gap of nearly a century, and a number of government reports and recommendations have followed the 1971 White Paper, *Better Services for the Mentally Handicapped*. During the 1970s the National Development Group published a series of pamphlets outlining models of service provision. The 1983 Mental Health Act has in the main taken mentally handicapped people out of mental health legislation unless they are mentally disordered as well as handicapped.

Sadly, the growth of the community care philosophy and moves toward integration are taking place at a time of economic restraint, and, as the "Panorama" programme *No Asylum* (BBC, 11 March 1985) demonstrated, there is increasing concern that community facilities will not keep pace with the closure of the Victorian institutions. Richard Titmuss' warning in 1968 still holds true that "we are drifting into a situation in which, by shifting the emphasis from the institution to the community — a trend which . . . we all applaud — we are transferring the care of the disabled from trained staff to untrained or ill-equipped staff, or no staff at all". And the Parliamentary Social Services Select Committee commented in January 1985: "The concept of asylum has nothing inherently to do with large or isolated institutions . . . *We must face the fact that some people need asylum*" (their italics)

DHSS statistics record a massive growth in the private care sector over the past seven years, and, without adequate public services and careful monitoring of private facilities, there is a danger of returning to the unlicensed "jungle" of the early 19th century, and that either an increase in society's fears or concern for the protection of mentally handicapped people could restart the cycle towards segregationist policies.

At present there are a number of projects designed to promote integration (see chapter 9) while, just as at the same stage in the last century, a number of charitable organisations have taken the opposite tack towards protection. The question raised by the 1908 Royal Commission on the Care of the Feeble-Minded (Radnor) is still being asked today, namely are mentally handicapped people fitted or unfitted to "take part in the struggle of life"?

Rothman, writing in 1971 about the founding of the American asylums in the 19th century, said: "We applaud the promoters of change, and are horrified with the results of their efforts". History has yet to make a judgement as to whether current policies will be a new beginning or merely a phase in a well-known cycle.

Reading

D. Wilkin (1979), *Caring for the Mentally Handicapped Child*, Chapter I, Croom Helm.

J. Ryan and F. Thomas (1980), *The Politics of Mental Handicap*, Penguin.

P. Morris (1969), *Put Away*, Routledge & Kegan Paul.

K. Jones (1972), *A History of the Mental Health Services*, Routledge & Kegan Paul.

K. Jones (1975), *Opening the Door*, Routledge and Kegan Paul.

A. Shearer (1980), *Handicapped Children in Residential Care: A Study of Policy Failure*, Bedford Square Press.

W. Wolfensberger (1975), *The Origin and Nature of our Institutional Models*, Human Policy Press (USA).

L. Kanner (1974), *A History of the Care and Study of the Mentally Retarded*, C.C. Thomas.

R. Titmuss (1968), *Commitment to Welfare*, Allen and Unwin.

D.J. Rothman (1971), *The Discovery of the Asylum*, Little, Brown and Co. (USA).

House of Commons Parliamentary Select Committee on Social Services (January 1985), *Community Care: with Special Reference to Adult Mentally Ill and Mentally Handicapped People*, Vol. 1, HMSO.

4

Causes of mental handicap

C linical conditions of mental handicap can be classified in a variety of ways, for example when they occur (prenatal, postnatal and so on) or under broad headings of causation (infections, physical trauma etc.). I have attempted to combine these as follows:

1) Prenatal
(a) *Mental handicap following infections*
For example:
(i) Congenital Rubella Syndrome. If the mother contracts Rubella (German Measles) in the first three months of pregnancy then damage to the foetus may result in mental handicap combined with sensory defects. Immunisation programmes for schoolgirls are reducing the incidence of what used to be one of the prime causes of mental handicap.
(ii) Toxoplasmosis. Infection transmitted to the foetus late in pregnancy and often resulting in Hydrocephalus or other more severe disabilities. A condition often linked to diet.
(iii) Congenital Syphilis
(iv) Cytomegalic Inclusion Disease
(b) *Physical*
(i) Poisoning through drug addiction, excessive alcohol consumption and smoking.
(ii) Intra-uterine irradiation
(iii) Injury to the mother
(iv) Rhesus incompatibility. This condition occurs if the mother is one of the 15 per cent of the population who is Rhesus negative and the foetus is the more usual Rhesus positive. Antibodies can cross the placenta and destroy the foetal red blood cells. With screening, treatment is available in utero.
(c) *Inherited*

A human being originates in the union of two sex cells and is built up of single cell units. Each cell is composed of cell membrane surrounding the complex cell structures. It is the cell nucleus which contains the hereditary material, chromosomes, in the form of strands of a material commonly known as DNA. This is the main compound of the chromosomes. Chromosomal disorders, such as in the addition of an extra chromosome to the normal complement of 46 (as in Down's Syndrome — Trisomy 21), or when an extra small chromosome attaches itself to another chromosome (Down's Syndrome — translocation).

The genes are a blueprint for the development of the individual Mental handicap caused by genetic disorders occurs as the result of a defective gene in one or both parents (dominant) or two similarly defective genes, one from each parent (recessive — that is, the parents are carriers). Some genetic disorders are sex-linked — for example, in Duchene Muscular Dystrophy, where both muscle wasting and mental retardation are present, females are the carriers, but only male children are affected.

Figure 6 *Mental handicap through inherited conditions*

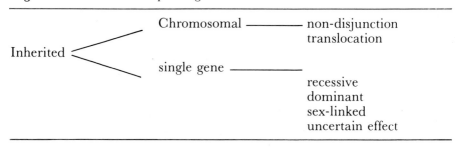

CHROMOSOMAL ABNORMALITIES

(i) Down's Syndrome: Regular (Trisomy 21), Translocation or Mosaic. Incidence — about 1:660 births and the most widely known mental handicap.

A high percentage of people with Down's have additional cardiac, respiratory and intestinal problems. Contrary to popular belief, character, intelligence and potential vary widely.

Incidence is linked with maternal age. Women over the age of 38 account for only three per cent of all pregnancies but for 23 per cent of all Down's children. American research in the past few years has, however, linked the syndrome to paternal age as well (K. Abrams and J. Binnet, "Current Findings in Down's Syndrome", *Exceptional Children*, 1983, 49:5).

(ii) *Cri de chat* Syndrome

(iii) Patau Syndrome (1:10,000 live births)

(iv) Sex Chromosome Abnormalities (for example Klinefelter's Syndrome: 1:500 live births. Turners Syndrome).

GENETIC ABNORMALITIES

(i) Microcephaly. Probably due to a single recessive gene which restricts brain size (1:1,000 live births).

(ii) Acrocephalosyndactyly

(iii) Tuberous Sclerosis (Epiloia), a condition caused by a single dominant gene with three major signs: mental retardation, epilepsy and a butterfly rash on the face. Tuberous growths appear in the brain and other organs. (1:20,000 live births).

(iv) Schilder's Disease.

(d) *Associated with metabolic disorders*

(i) Disorders of lipid metabolism

(ii) Disorders of amino-acid metabolism — for example, Phenylketonuria, a very damaging condition which affects many functions but can now be detected by the Guthrie test and contained by diet (1:12,000 births).

(iii) Disorders of carbohydrate metabolism — for example, Holer's Syndrome (Gargoylism)

(iv) Disorders of endocrine metabolism — for example, Cretinism.

(2) Perinatal

(a) *Problems in late pregnancy* — for example, eclampsia.

(b) *Problems associated with prematurity.*

(i) Cerebral Palsy (1:500 live births) is a permanent disorder of movement and posture caused by a non-progressive defect of the brain occurring in early life. The condition does not necessarily mean mental handicap but usually causes permanent hemiplegia or even quadraplegia sometimes with athetoid movements. Epilepsy is common.

(ii) Kernicterus

(c) *Birth injury* through direct physical damage, brain haemorrhage or anoxia (oxygen starvation).

(d) *Metabolic disorders.*

(i) Hypoglycaemia — low blood sugar in the new born may cause impairment

(ii) Hypercalcaemia (William's Syndrome) — an excess of blood calcium

(3) Postnatal

(a) *Following infection*

(i) Meningitis

(ii) Encephalitis is an infection of the brain tissue and may occur following infection with measles, rubella, chicken pox etc. In young infants the effects may be more severe than those of many inherited disorders.

(b) *Following reaction to vaccination*, for example, brain damage following vaccination for whooping cough.

(c) *Sensory and social deprivation*

A large number of children with moderate learning difficulties are held back not by an intrinsic clinical condition but by inadequate stimulation or a sensory deprivation which impedes their ability to absorb knowledge and develop concepts.

(d) *Physical*

(i) Road accidents

(ii) Non-accidental injury (child abuse)

(iii) Poisons — for example, lead poisoning

(4) Other Conditions

(a) *Epilepsy* — Many well known historical figures have had epilepsy (for example, Julius Caesar, St Paul and Tchaikovsky) and there is no automatic connection with mental handicap. The word epilepsy is derived from the

Greek *epi lambano*, meaning "a taking hold of". Handicapping conditions can, however, cause epilepsy and status epilepticus can cause brain damage. Epilepsy can cause personality difficulties, and many mildly mentally handicapped people are more handicapped by their epilepsy than their intellectual retardation.

(b) *Mental illness*

(i) Childhood Autism. Approximately 70–80 per cent of autistic children are mildly or severely retarded with the additional problems of a difficulty in forming relationships, ritualistic behaviour and often speech abnormalities, (L. Wing "Management of Early Autism", *British Journal of Hospital Medicine*, Vol. 25 No. 4, 1981).

(ii) Adult Psychosis can sometimes cause such a severe loss of functioning as to necessitate assistance from the mental handicap services.

(iii) There is some evidence that there is more likelihood of a child being born handicapped if the mother is suffering from a psychotic illness in pregnancy (see research by L. Heston (1966) in the *British Journal of Psychiatry*, Vol. 112, pp819–825).

Figure 7 *Developmental stages*

Development stage	Conception	birth	1 yr	2 yrs	3 yrs	10 yrs	16 yrs
Group	Prenatal	Perinatal					
		—————— POSTNATAL ——————					

(from D. Clarke, 1982)

Approximately 65 per cent of all cases of mental handicap remain undefined. Factors may be genetic or a mixture of genetic and environmental. A specific diagnosis does not usually mean that there could be a "cure" but parents do find a label useful to enable them to come to terms and to plan ahead.

NB It is difficult to classify handicapping conditions as well recognised signs and symptoms can often occur for different reasons. Hydrocephaly, for example, can be caused by a recessive gene in the female chromosome or as the result of meningitis. Microcephaly is a condition in its own right but may occur as a factor in other syndromes as well.

Reading

C. Hallas *et al* (1982) *The Care and Training of the Mentally Handicapped*, Wright — PSG.

D. Clarke (1982), *Mentally Handicapped People: Living and Learning*, Part 2, Baillière Tindall.

M. Craft, J. Bicknell, S. Hollins (eds) (1985), *Mental Handicap: A Multidisciplinary Approach*, Section 3, Baillière Tindall.

C. Cunningham (1982), *Down's Syndrome: An Introduction for Parents*, Souvenir Press.

For a brief description of individual syndromes see L. Holmes *et al* (1972), *Mental Retardation: An Atlas of Diseases with Associated Physical Abnormalities*, Macmillan.

For a list of parent support groups for those with specific syndromes — the only up-to-date publication is by Ann Worthington (1984) *Useful addresses for Parents with a Handicapped Child* available from Mrs Worthington, 10 Norman Road, Sale, Cheshire M33 3DF. See also *Glossary of Terms* available from the same address.

Informative articles on particular syndromes appear in the journal *Adoption and Fostering* published by the British Association of Agencies for Fostering and Adoption and in the National Children's Bureau "Highlights" series. (See appendix I below, "Useful names and addresses".)

5
The effects of disability

"All cases of absolute inequality among men", wrote the distinguished blind scholar, Pierre Villey, "engender vices". Those with a disability often have the humiliation of asking for help with basic necessities and the helper is placed in a position of disproportionate power that is helpful to the moral position of neither.

Mentally handicapped people are often given a "mess of pottage" ("care") only in return for their "birthright" ("citizenship"). Until 1983 residents in mental handicap hospitals on a voluntary basis could not vote. Often they are given no say in their everyday life style: what they shall wear or eat. Many people are allowed no choice as to their living environment, but are moved for administrative convenience.

Figure 8 *Common experiences of mentally handicapped people*

Negative image	—	Avoidance. Low expectations. Fear. Segregation.
Damaged relationships	—	Rejection. Discontinuity of care. Distance.
Powerlessness	—	Low autonomy. Insecurity.
Low economy	—	Financial poverty and poverty of experience.
Frustration	—	Lack of communication and access to change.

The example of Joey Deacon at St Lawrence's Hospital, Caterham, Surrey is a potent one. Joey's spasticity and consequent poor articulation ensured that he was labelled as "low grade". It was a fellow resident, a close friend, who discovered that Joey had a keen mind and had something to say once it could be interpreted, a disabled person, not a member of staff who unlocked the door to Joey's prison.

Because a disabled person may experience difficulty in expressing his emotions or may show them in an unfamiliar manner, it is sometimes easy to take this for a lack of real feeling. As a social worker with a mentally handicapped person facing a situation of deprivation, it is important to assume that the emotional effect will be as strong for the client as anyone else, while the emotional response is likely to be dependent on additional factors.

Figure 9 *Negative career pattern*

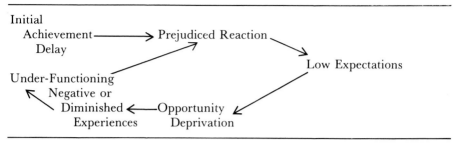

(From A. Tyne (1981) The Principle of Normalisation, CMH)

For instance, in bereavement the usual process of shock, denial, searching, despair and reorientation may be complicated by additional factors:

☐ The unusual dependence on a parental figure.
☐ A "conspiracy of protection" by relatives.
☐ The denial of visual images (for example, attendance at the funeral) to aid grief.
☐ The lack of a close friend to share feelings with.
☐ Difficulties in comprehension and communication.
☐ A change in environment and life-style if the loss results in admission to residential care.

The counsellor can be aware that as in other areas of development the mentally handicapped person may get "stuck" in one phase and so there is a need for the bereaved to be guided through the grief process.

In the case of young children the very useful accent on early learning can mean children being placed in special schools at the age of two years, rather than domiciliary teaching or playgroups being provided — with the consequent effect of maternal separation. At the most vital level of the right to life and to treatment, some handicapped people are denied basic treatment because of a subjective evaluation of their condition, or subjected to extraordinary means to preserve their existence.

In 1975 the United Nations made a declaration on the rights of disabled people and since then people have added or adapted these according to circumstances:-

☐ *The right to life*, the prime right on which everything else depends. The "Arthur Case" of 1982 threw into sharp relief the ethical issues concerning the value we place on human life. As a society we need to consider whether we should, with all our material resources and medical knowledge, adopt the Spartan approach of exposing disabled infants. If we decide to opt for life then we must concern ourselves with the quality of that life.

- *The right to childhood* and a family in which to develop.
- *The right to proper assessment* and continuing medical care and treatment.
- *The right of access to generic services* as well as any specialist services which might be needed.
- *The right to take part* in the rhythms of ordinary life.
- *The right to take risks*, make choices and take the consequences of personal decisions.
- *The right to a decent living* and security.
- *The right not to overburden their families*, and in adulthood to be free from parental decision-making.
- *The right to leave home* and live in ordinary housing.
- *The right to an independent guardian* to protect his or her interests.
- *The right to work* and acquire leisure skills and activities.
- *The right to friendships*, to privacy, personal achievement and sexuality.

These rights raise the question of whether parents or the individuals themselves are the client. This is not only a moral issue but a practical one, as parents who have cared for their offspring for many years are naturally resistant to strangers talking about ''independence''. This issue can only be realistically faced by good early work with families on the basis of partnership.

Reading
J. Bicknell (1983), ''Mentally Handicapped People: Their Rights and Responsibilities'', *British Journal of Occupational Therapy*, 46, 6.
P. Mittler *op cit*, Chapter 1.
D. Thomas (1982), *The Experience of Handicap.* Methuen.
E. Hastings (1981), ''The Experience of Disability'', *Australian Journal of Developmental Disabilities*, 7, 3.
J. Deacon (1974), *Tongue Tied*, MENCAP.
M. Oswin (1981), *Bereavement and Mentally Handicapped People*, King's Fund.

6
The mentally handicapped person and his family

Expectations

I t has been said that in the months preceding birth the mother will experience many subconscious and primeval fears relating to the safety of the child. If the infant is whole then the fears evaporate, if not ...
Parents and their kin have expectations. Comments such as "my husband really wanted a boy ..." are often heard outside the school gates. People desire a child who looks like them, who will do the things they like doing, who may achieve the goals they strived for but never attained.

Crisis

The crisis of handicap (see Figure 12) is likely to occur at or shortly after birth, but can occur at any time. In chapter 4 we looked at various

Figure 10 *Effects of Differential Identification*

Group	Examples of conditions	Comments
Impairments which are obvious to everyone at birth.	Some hydrocephalies, almost all spina bifidas and skeletal and limb deformities.	Shock for parents with possible rejection. Need for immediate treatment may affect bonding.
Conditions that may be apparent to the doctor and midwife but not to the parents.	Down's Syndrome and other chromosomal abnormalities, some cerebral palsies and microcephaly.	Paediatrician has to decide when to tell the parents: too soon may provoke rejection, too long an interval may induce anxiety.
Conditions where the disabling factor is slow to occur.	Epilepsy, most cerebral palsies, metabolic disorders and sensory impairment	Family may "slip through the net" of assessment and support. Onus for the identification of the handicap may fall on the parents themselves.

Group	Examples of conditions	Comments
Impairment caused by trauma.	*Vaccine damage, accident or poisoning.*	*Rejection is unlikely to occur with this group as bonding has already taken place.*
		Parents may get less support and are faced with the "loss" of a child they have grown to love.

classifications of mental handicap, but it can also be useful to look at this from the point of view of when the impairment is identified

Parents' Reactions to the Crisis

Many books have been written recently by parents about their feelings, and these can perhaps be seen most clearly in the following schema, adapted from the work of Dr. Ronald McKeith, which outlines the range of often very contradictory feelings that parents may experience and their consequent behaviour.

Figure 11   *Responses to the birth of a handicapped child*

Reaction	Behaviour
Biological (a) Protection of the helpless.	— warm normal care. — highly protective care.
(b) Revulsion at the abnormal.	— cold rejection. — rationalised rejection. — dutiful caring. — lavish over-compensation.

"I felt sick when he told me. I looked at the baby and I could see it ... I could see the mongol look ... I didn't want to touch him ..." (quoted in Cunningham, 1982).

Reaction	Behaviour
Feelings of Inadequacy (a) Inadequacy at reproduction	— loss of self respect. — depression.
(b) Inadequacy in rearing.	— lack of confidence and hence inconsistency in child rearing.

"After another futile attempt to feed Will I drove home feeling terribly depressed. I sat half way up the stairs and cried. I felt a total failure. I had failed to produce a normal child: 'Almost anyone can produce a normal child', I thought, but I can't and I can't even feed him" (Boston, 1981).

Reaction	Behaviour

Bereavement at the loss of the normal child.

(a) Anger	— aggression towards spouse, family and professionals.
(b) Grief	— depression
(c) Adjustment	— anger and grief need to be worked through

"I felt I *should* be angry and depressed ... there may be something very wrong with my baby. To be well adjusted in this situation is absolutely crazy". (Kupfer, 1982).

Shock	— disbelief and a search for a more favourable diagnosis.
	— denial of the impairment.

"I can't recall what we were told on that occasion. An awful lot of what he [the paediatrician] said was lost. I had already begun to look out of the window. The feeling I had was that the roof was coming in on us". (quoted in Burton, 1975)

Panic	— a temporary reaction to an unknown situation, but a strategy that can become a permanent way of "coping".

"Not normal, not normal. My mind struggled with this alien concept, but could not grasp it. I felt buffeted by meaningless words which were heavy with menace. The voice went on, as though the world was still the same: 'He has Höhler's Syndrome, a rare disease. In English you call it...-er, gargoylism.'

"Through the thickening fog in my head I heard him, and into my punch-drunk consciousness swam hideous figures, straight off the pages of *Notre Dame de Paris* — gargoyles. Monstrous creatures carved in stone, water gushing out of their leering mouths. Oh God, not that; anything but that. Not my son." (Craig, 1979)

Guilt	— not always experienced and often alleviated by good genetic counselling.
	— depression
	— sublimation

"Sometimes I wondered whether his condition had some personal relationship with my relationship with God — a sort of chastisement" (quoted in Burton, 1975).

Embarrassment Shame, panic and guilt coupled with the extra time needed for practical tasks can lead to	— social withdrawal and isolation.

"For four months I never went out of the house, not even to the shops. I just cut myself off from everybody" (parent taking to author).

"It's segregation of parents; you ought to have integration of parents, let alone integration of children ..." (quoted in Glendinning, 1983).

Crisis intervention

What Cunningham terms the "psychic crisis" of having a handicapped child is likely to follow a fairly well-defined pattern and professionals can learn to respond in helpful ways.

Figure 12 *Model of psychic crisis at disclosure of handicap*

PARENT IS TOLD		*Manifestations*		*Needs*
	SHOCK PHASE	Emotional disorganization, confusion, paralysis of actions, disbelief, irrationality	Can last from 2 minutes to several days	Empathy and emotional support
Frequent oscillation between phases	REACTION PHASE	Expression of: sorrow, grief, disappointment, anxiety, aggression, denial, guilt, failure, defence mechanisms	A process of reintegration through discussion	Listen to parent. Catharsis through talking out Sympathy but honesty Facts on cause
	ADAPTATION PHASE	Realistic appraisal: parents ask "What can be done?" This is a *signal of readiness* to proceed with 'How can we help?'		Reliable and accurate information on medical and educational treatment and future
	ORIENTATION PHASE	Parents begin to organize, seek help and information, plan for future		Provision of regular help and guidance in treatment
	IMMEDIATE CRISIS OVER			Appropriate provision of services

From: C. Cunningham, "Parent Counselling" in M Craft (ed) (1979), Tredgold's Mental Retardation, 12th Edition, Baillière Tindall.

"The lost child lives on"

Although, as Figure 12 suggests, good professional intervention can help parents surmount the immediate crisis, there is little doubt that, as one commentator put it, "the lost child lives on", or in Olshansky's well-known phrase, parents suffer from "chronic sorrow".

As neighbouring children start school, go into work or training schemes, marry and start a family, the parents' sense of loss recurs, sometimes with increasing intensity. As one parent graphically portrayed her feelings:

"At least the act, the death, is an ending ... and the parents' wounds can begin to heal. I feel as if I am always re-enacting Kathleen's death. As she becomes older and less appealing, her problems become more pronounced. When we go back to the neurologist, when I go to her special class for evaluation, I feel as if the coffin is being wheeled in again'' (quoted in Kupfer, 1982).

The effect on family relationships

Although some studies have linked an increasing rate of marital breakdown with having a handicapped child, it is probably more accurate to say with Gath (*Down's Syndrome and the Family: The Early Years*, Academic Press, 1978) that the advent of a handicapped child is ''. . . not as likely to mar a good marriage as to turn a moderate or somewhat shaky marriage into a poor one. The unhappily married were most often those who had experienced considerable conflict, shown by hiding the new born mongol away or wanting to leave it in hospital or considering leaving the neighbourhood . . .''

Clearly there are enormous psychological and physical strains facing the family as a whole, which need sound relationships and excellent communication to avoid fracture or the development of pathological coping mechanisms. As Fox described the work facing families as ''an ambivalent conflict between acceptance of the unacceptable and rejection of the clearly real'' (quoted in Hollins, 1985), so the effects on the family may result in:

- [ ] Social stigma and isolation of the family or some members of it.
- [ ] Lack of understanding and alienation from the extended family.
- [ ] Shattered expectations leading to pressure on the other siblings.
- [ ] Renegotiation of family roles.
- [ ] An increased burden of daily care and ''ambassadorial'' functions falling on the mother.
- [ ] The mentally handicapped person becoming an ''eternal child'' or an over-vital stalwart in the parents' old age.

Mothers and fathers

Much of the burden of care will fall on the mother, and, as the child's development is delayed, the woman's aim of fulfilling her potential as a child-rearer (see Glendinning, 1983, p41) as well as a career person is seriously imperilled. As Mary Craig recalls: ''Once I had thought of myself as a woman with intellectual interests, but now my life was focused entirely on Paul . . . he was a round-the-clock, full-time job'' (Craig, 1979).

The modern trend for fathers of all social classes to be more involved should be a support for mothers, but differing perspectives combined with the tendency of professionals to relate primarily to the mother, may be increasingly damaging to the marital relationship and ultimately to the well-being of the child. Despite a move towards shared ways of handling children mothers tend to be concerned mainly with day-to-day issues, while fathers look to the future (see also Cunningham 1982, p55), and may suffer from unresolved grief. One research project on fathers found that only 10 per cent of fathers had seen a paediatric social worker, and only 20 per cent an area social worker. Fathers of children with Down's Syndrome were more inclined to opt out of family life than those with multiply handicapped children.

The author concludes:

"... the majority of fathers suffer chronic sorrow which continues undiminished as the child grows older. In view of this, professional workers should not expect the father to carry the burden of supporting his wife, but on the contrary they should offer the father the same sort of support which is given to the mother". (J. Rodhouse (1982), *Child Handicap and the Family: The Father as the Focus for Research*, MSW thesis, University of Sussex).

Sexual relations can be adversely affected by the advent of a handicapped child. The feelings surrounding the woman's wholeness and creativity and the father's virility, the fear of pregnancy aroused by the dread of having another handicapped child, or the desire to devote all energies to the child already born, may cause the sexual part of the relationship to decline (J. Tizard and J.C. Grad (1961), *The Mentally Handicapped and Their Families*, Oxford University Press). Because of their nocturnal activity many handicapped children sleep with their parents. As one parent said: "He sleeps with me because if he didn't he'd be in and out of bed all night . . . He sleeps alright. He kicks a bit" (quoted in Glendinning, 1983).

Not all is gloom, however. Many parents feel more united as a couple through their experiences and so many have a particular kind of what we might call "trench humour", that particular brand of ironic humour that comes in adversity. A sound developmental programme worked out with both parents (for example, The Portage Developmental Checklist or that outlined in C. Cunningham and P. Sloper (1978), *Helping Your Handicapped Baby*, Souvenir Press) should help both parents and child as long as it is well supported by professionals, allows for negative feelings, and lets parents enjoy their baby as a baby first and handicapped second.

Brothers and sisters

Although the pressure of a child in the family whose slow development abnormally prolongs his childhood is bound to affect the siblings, the effect need not necessarily be wholly negative. Owens and Birchenall see brothers and sisters as mainly following their parents' attitudes, and many feelings may be influenced by the handicapped child's position in the family. Hannam records that in one of the families he interviewed, Philip's brothers and sisters wouldn't allow his parents to place him in residential care during the family holiday:

"There is a great cry of 'if he were normal you wouldn't dream of doing that' . . . We wouldn't dare put him in for a holiday because they adore playing with him on the sands" (quoted in Hannam, 1975).

While many parents feel unable to discipline their handicapped child, and fathers especially may retreat from this sphere (see Hewett 1970, chapter 4), other parents will have been advised to exert a firmer control. Either approach may cause a reaction in the siblings, who feel resentful at favouritism shown to another or insecure at their parents' lack of

Table 4 *Changes in sibling attitude towards a sick child*

Changes in attitude to the illness	Older Siblings %	Younger Siblings %
Gives in more easily to sick child	43	12
Less aggressive than otherwise	46	12
Feels protective towards sick child	57	19
Feels responsible for sick child's wellbeing	43	12
Feels jealous of attention received by sick child	22	29
Feels worried about the illness	47	9
Talks to or taunts sick child about illness	8	12

(From Burton, 1975)

consistency.

Although parents were often in the past advised to have their handicapped infant "put away in an institution" for the sake of the family, this may be counterproductive: "Indeed the air of mystery that can surround an institutionalised child may have a deleterious effect on children still at home" (O. Rowlands (1982), "Down's Syndrome and the Family", *Adoption and Fostering*, Vol. 6 No. 1).

If a child has to go into residential care then it is best that the move is discussed with the other children so that they are not left bewildered or fearing that they too may be sent away if they are "difficult". As Fern Kupfer's daughter points out to her friends, "We are *not* all here . . . Zachy is not here!" (Kupfer, 1982).

Grandparents and the wider network

The literature tends to be rather gloomy about the response of grandparents and the wider community. Certainly the husband's 'phone call from hospital with the news can destroy many fond hopes. Many grandparents question the diagnosis at the time, others may show undue optimism or pessimism; in a few cases grandparents "arranged residential care before the mother and baby even get out of hospital" (Cunningham, 1982, pp47–52).

In many families, however, at least one grandparent rallies round and sometimes they are the only support — "The only person who will babysit is Mum" (quoted in Glendinning, 1983, see pp99–105). Regarding other members of the extended family and the wider social network, research studies disagree as to how accepting and actively helpful neighbourhoods may be. Bayley (1973) found that his Sheffield families received considerable support from relatives (70 per cent) and neighbours (74 per cent). Wilkins (1979), however, decided that the contribution of persons other than parents was "almost negligible". Glendinning balances these influential surveys by surmising that the degree of outside help may depend on the stage in the family's life-cycle and mutual perception of "need" and "help".

What is clear is that social services must strive to complement not contradict, informal support networks. Official and unofficial help should be seen as "complementary and inextricably interwoven" (Bayley, 1973) so that statutory services strengthen the network of support created by the families themselves.

The "daily grind"

Where there is a severe developmental delay parents often face what Michael Bayley called the "daily grind" of care. The ordinary problems of everyday living are magnified and a sense of weariness may develop from particular problems such as sleep disturbance:

> "He won't stop in bed, he is in and out of bed all night, so he's been sleeping with my husband, and I sleep in his bed" (quoted in Bayley, 1973)

or the sense of unending caring:

> "And you know unless something alters very radically we're going to continue this way. That's the frightening thing . . . I can see me being this way in five or six years time" (quoted in Glendinning, 1983).

Sheila Hewett's study, published in 1970, looking at families with young children suffering from cerebral palsy (of whom about 55 per cent are mentally handicapped) demonstrates the immense problems of physical management involved in daily care (see table 5).

Butler's survey in Bristol in 1979 confirms this picture. Two-thirds of the children at ESN(s) schools were dependent on their families for one aspect of self care; 40 per cent were incontinent; a third needed attention at least once a night; and 45 per cent of parents had problems in taking the child out (N. Butler *et al.* (1978), *Handicapped Children: Their Homes and Lifestyles*, University of Bristol).

Such cares not only put strain on the mothers, but evidence suggests that, in the case of multiply handicapped children especially, fathers make economic and social sacrifices to help in the caring tasks (Hunter, 1980). Hunter also records that over half of the parents in her study suffered chronic ill-health.

Parental health

"I felt that depressed yesterday", recalls a parent in conversation with Caroline Glendinning, "I could have sat and cried all day".

All research studies have shown an adverse effect on families' physical and psychological health unless practical and emotional sustenance was offered and accepted. Gath's survey of mothers with Down's children showed a 33 per cent rate of depression within 18 months of the birth of the child, twice as high as the controls. (A. Gath (1978), *Down's Syndrome and the Family: The Early Years*, Academic Press).

The mothers in Wilkin's study reported symptoms of frequent colds, lethargy, and chronic conditions such as back pain and rheumatism. 72 per cent of the mothers experienced feelings of emotional weariness, of "being nervy, on edge or depressed".

Economic factors

The Family Fund survey of 1974 found that coping with a handicapped dependant means considerable financial sacrifices for about 90 per cent of parents. This has been confirmed by Hunter in 1980 and most recently in Judith Buckle's survey in 1984 for the Disablement Income Group. Buckle suggests that having a mentally handicapped dependant can cost a family £3,198 per year. The example of "Jenny Smith", given in the survey, shows graphically how benefits such as Mobility Allowance are needed well before the age of entitlement (see Table 6).

Table 5 *Incidence of disabilities/management problems*

	No. of children	%
Unable to sit at all without support	56	31
Unable to walk at all	69	38
Functional mobility nil	56	31
Functional mobility confined to one room	11	6
Unable to put on clothes without help	124	69
Unable to feed himself without help	67	37
Unable to drink from a cup/uses feeding bottle	32	18
Difficulty with chewing and/or swallowing	63	35
Doubly incontinent	67	38
Impairment of vision (known to mother)	66	36
Impairment of hearing (known to mother)	15	8
Impairment of speech: 1 slight/moderate	31	17
2 serious	21	12
3 can say 1–2 words only	27	15
4 no speech	52	29
Sleeping problems: 1 getting to sleep	52	29
2 waking often during night	18	10
3 waking sometimes during night	96	53
Fits/convulsions	44	24

(*Hewett, 1970*)

The Family Fund discovered that only 24 per cent of their survey mothers could get out to work, against a national average of 40 per cent. Quite often fathers sacrifice overtime to help in the care or refuse promotion so as to keep the handicapped child in a settled situation. Forty per cent of the fathers Burton (1975) interviewed felt that their work had been interfered with or negatively influenced. Many felt deprived of the opportunity to care for their child. As one father put it, "Every day at work I ponder what is going to happen — studying this and that. You can't say you're a free man".

Table 6 *The economic consequences of handicap*

Household with one adult, two children
JENNY SMITH, aged 2½
Disability: Microcephaly and cerebral palsy
Household composition: Lives with divorced mother and sibling
Tenure: Local authority housing
Income: Gross normal weekly household income is 101% of that of an average
household of similar composition[1]

Summary of income and expenditure	£
Total gross weekly household income	101.45
Total weekly ongoing extra costs of mental handicap	2.00
Capitl costs of mental handicap	2.00
Weekly loss of earnings of mother	60.00
Social security benefits as % of weekly household income[2]	72%
Weekly extra costs as % of household income	29%

Capital costs (1981 prices) of mental handicap	£
Mattress cover (1981)	2

Weekly household income	£
Attendance allowance	23.65
Child benefit	10.50
Child benefit increase	3.30
Supplementary benefit	36.00
Maintenance	24
Mother's earnings	4.00
TOTAL	101.45

Ongoing extra costs of mental handicap	£
General increase in housekeeping costs	50
Unprescribed medication	50
Transport to creche at hospital	90
Taxi fares	256
Extra telephone calls	100
Disposable nappies	216
Waterproof pants	48
Toiletries for incontinence	78
Extra bedding	60
Extra laundry costs	36

Capital costs (1981 prices) of mental handicap		Ongoing extra costs of mental handicap	
		Extra clothing costs	55
		Wasted food	100
		Extra gas and electricity	286
		Extra wear & tear around the house	50
		Extra spent on other child to "compensate"	50
TOTAL	2	TOTAL	1,525

(From J. Buckle, 1984)

Differentials in handicap

We all tend to think that our own life experience is the one most fraught with difficulty, but groups of parents sharing together quickly agree that each degree of disability brings its very particular challenges and rewards. The severely multiply handicapped child requires many minute attentions throughout the day and night; the very mobile child may be just as physically tiring as parents try and anticipate him rushing towards open windows and across roads; the person who doesn't look handicapped will often meet expectations of achievement and behaviour from the public which she cannot meet.

Persons with additional sensory handicaps are at an extra disadvantage. Some of the most inappropriately placed people are those who have some degree of retardation but are also blind and/or deaf. Christopher Brock, a victim of rubella syndrome, was profoundly deaf, partially sighted and with a moderate learning difficulty, was admitted temporarily to a mental handicap hospital because no appropriate placement in the community could be found. Christopher's mother found that " . . . the fact of their treble handicap . . . disqualifies them for places within the other disciplines" (M. Brock (1984), *Christopher: A Silent Life*, Bedford Square Press).

Some parents with children suffering from combined mental and physical disabilities find insufficient help from the statutory services and turn to intensive home-based developmental programmes such as the Doman Delacato System (G. Doman (1974), *What to do about your Brain-Injured Child*, Jonathan Cape). In some instances the programmes devised at the institute in Philadelphia or its English equivalent at Bridgwater can achieve astonishing results (see L. Scotson (1985), *Doran: Child of Courage*, Collins); for others it can mean years of struggle with no measureable progress. For some families the requirement for a number of neighbourhood helpers to provide constant stimulation creates many firm friendships, (A. Jones and F. Owen (1984), *Handle with Care*, Gresham Books); for others the concentration on the handicapped member can create resentment and lasting harm.

So-called "M" children, those with what the 1981 Education Act terms a "moderate learning difficulty", are provided for by special schools (what were previously termed ESN(m) schools) but they and their families are often forgotten by social services.

Many "M" children are not truly handicapped but placed in an administrative category because their social circumstances have produced a learning difficulty — a situation recognised by the 1981 Act. There are, however, a number of children with a recognised handicap (for example, Down's Syndrome, at "M" schools). Parents have often fought hard to have their children placed away from what were called ESN(s) schools and are naturally upset if a later assessment recommends a placement in a "S" school, or when leaving school, the only opportunity available is within clearly designated mental handicap provision (for example, an adult training centre) . A good social work strategy should encompass this group of children and their families so that they are not forgotten.

A sense of proportion

The mental health departments, which existed before the 1971 Seebohm reorganisation of social services, tended to focus on the handicapped person, what Simon Kew (1975) calls the "concentric approach". Recently the needs of parents were focussed on, and now the rights of the handicapped individual are being stressed almost as determinedly counter to those of the parents.

In reality what is needed is a sense of proportion with the balance of rights and the needs of parent and offspring illuminated by child care philosophy and the dignity of the handicapped person.

As the BASW Charter states:

> "Children's rights and needs do not exist in a vacuum. They are bound up with those of their parents ... While children's rights and parents' rights are entirely complementary and to a large extent indivisible, parental rights are NOT rights of possession and they do not take precedence over the child's right to an upbringing which will promote his emotional, physical, social and intellectual well-being" (*Social Work Today*, 1977, Vol 8, No. 25).

Many types of respite care schemes have been developed in recent years, ranging from reserved beds on hospital wards to linking families in local neighbourhoods. At their best respite schemes can give the handicapped child new experiences and friendships while enabling the parents to have a break and spend time with their other children. Maureen Oswin's recent study (1984), however, shows that there are dangers both in residential and quasi-fostering schemes if they are not based on sound child care principles.

Many parents, as they grow older, become very dependent on their handicapped "child". Cunningham (1982) recalls a 28 year old woman with Down's Syndrome telling him that: "They [her parents] still won't let me get my own place. I look after them too well. I do all the shopping and tidying. They'd be lost without me".

Social workers cannot expect, however, to descend from above and sever an umbilical cord that has lasted for many years. By responding early to parents needs social workers will ultimately have more chance of securing the individual's rights.

Substitute families

A study of Down's Syndrome children born in 1970/1 in one health region, showed that 10 per cent required substitute care (A. Gath (1983), "Mentally Retarded Children in Substitute and Natural Families", *Adoption and Fostering*, Vol. 7 No. 1.)

Rejected handicapped infants are more likely to be put forward for fostering and adoption, and the needs of these substitute families should not be ignored.

Gath states that the separation of the emotional trauma of giving birth to a handicapped child from the practical problems of caring, and the element of choosing to care, can make these placements very successful. Good pre-placement work, bringing in the families' children, can also produce good positive results, as Gath records: "A high risk of joining the 'caring professions' appears to be a characteristic of young people who have been brought up with handicapped children"!

Substitute parents may feel various pressures, however:
- [ ] The need to develop the child's "full potential" can result in an over-emphasis on developmental programmes with resultant strain on parent and child.
- [ ] The desire for respite from the day-to-day care may be guilt-inducing.
- [ ] The substitute family may feel that they have to give "life care" and this could result in the mentally handicapped child losing opportunities for independence.

Foster families are likely to have their needs reviewed through the child care system, but adoptive parents should be offered the same support as natural parents of a mentally handicapped child.

The future

While most parents can shepherd their child's development to the age of majority and then watch him gain more independence, the parents of a mentally handicapped child will always worry about his vulnerability long into adulthood, perhaps for ever.

Residential care is not always an answer either, as changes in policy within the NHS or social services create apprehension about change and raise the fear among older parents of having to pick up the reins of coping again, or provide for a permanent representative (see G. Sanctuary (1984) *After I'm Gone: What will Happen to my Handicapped Child*, Souvenir Press). The guilt of asking other people to share the burden of care also means the burden itself is never really relinquished. As the parents in BBC 1's *The Visit* (1983) said of placing their child, Jemima, in a residential centre: "It's a sort of dying . . . We feel like partners in a criminal conspiracy . . . and we can't talk about the crime".

Separation may be the ultimate parting of death. The death of a child whose handicap made her even more dependent is unendurable, and the momentary pang of relief at the lifting of a life-long anxiety is likely to produce feelings of guilt. Social work responsibility should not end at the death of the handicapped person. When Sarah Boston's Down's Syndrome son died she had to rely on self-help therapy, though what she needed was "someone who knew about grief, who knew the stages, whom I could talk to and who could advise me" (Boston, 1981).

Conclusion

While it would be wrong not to portray the real difficulties faced by families with a handicapped member, it can be both dangerous and inaccurate to paint a completely negative picture. Maureen Oswin, in her research on short-term care services (M. Oswin (1984), *They Keep Going Away*, Kings Fund/Oxford University Press), criticises social workers for falling into a trap of seeing children with mental handicap as primarily a burden on their parents rather than a child with strong family relationships.

For many parents the bond between them and their child is deeper because of the handicap: "Part of me is gone when he goes there [the hostel] for a couple of nights" (quoted in Oswin, 1984).

Some find the experience is an unexpected pathway to growth. As Frances Young writes: "Arthur is a focus of care and affection. He has been the catalyst of significant discoveries about human relationships. He has helped us all to a greater maturity" (F. Young (1985), *Face to Face*, Epworth Press).

Others share a sense of achievement that we might overlook, as in the case of a mother whose child raised money for a local youth club with a sponsored swim: "After being told one's child would be a 'loveable cabbage' I watched her swim and wanted to shout that even one small talent can achieve something, and that our children can give something back however small" (quoted in Worthington, 1982).

All the surveys show that having a handicapped person in the family has profound emotional, practical and psychological effects. If you are strong already then the experience can develop those strengths, if there are weaknesses then it will seek them out. The social worker's main resource is her own humanity in combining empathy, a working partnership and practical action in situations which may have common factors but are in essence quite unique.

The terrible double-bind which often we place parents in is that we expect them to struggle on on their own for years and years unaided and then criticise them for not letting go when we professionals judge the time is right. An example to be followed is that shown in the BBC film *Cathy Leaves Home* where families and professionals worked together to face change in a positive and affirming manner.

Reading

S. Hewett (1970), *The Family and the Handicapped Child*, Allen & Unwin.

G. Owens and P. Birchenall (1979), *Mental Handicap: The Social Dimensions*, Pitman Medical.

C. Cunningham (1982), *Down's Syndrome: An Introduction for Parents*, Souvenir Press.

C. Glendinning (1983), *Unshared Care: Parents and Their Disabled Children*, Routledge & Kegan Paul.

S. Kew (1975), *Handicap and Family Crisis*, Pitman.

R. McKeith (1974), "The Feelings and Behaviour of Parents of Handicapped children", in D. Boswell and J. Wingrove, *The Handicapped Person in the Community*, Tavistock.

C. Hannam (1975), *Parents and Mentally Handicapped Children*, Penguin/MIND.

S. Boston (1981), *Will, My Son*, Pluto Press.

F. Kupfer (1982), *Before and After Zachariah*, Gollancz.

A. Worthington (1982), *Coming to Terms with Mental Handicap*, Helena Press.

L. Burton (1975), *The Family Life of Sick Children*, Routledge & Kegan Paul.

M. Philip and D. Duckworth (1982), *Children with Disabilities and their Families*, NFER-Nelson.

E. Browne (1982), *Mental Handicap: The Role for Social Workers*, University of Sheffield/*Community Care* Monograph.

M. Oswin (1984), *They Keep Going Away*, King's Fund/Oxford University Press.

J. Buckle (1984), *Mental Handicap Costs More*, Disablement Income Group.

S. Hollins (1985), "Families and Handicap" in M. Craft, J. Bicknell and S. Hollins (ed), *Mental Handicap: A Multi-Disciplinary Approach*, Baillière Tindall.

D. Anderson (1982), *Social Work and Mental Handicap*, MacMillan.

A. Hunter (1980), *The Family and Their Mentally Handicapped Child*, Barnardo Paper No. 12.

M. Bayley (1973), *Mental Handicap and Community Care*, Routledge & Kegan Paul.

D. Wilkin (1979), *Caring for the Mentally Handicapped Child*, Croom Helm.

M. Craig (1979), *Blessings*, Hodder and Stoughton.

S. Olshansky (1920), "Chronic Sorrow: A response to having a mentally defective child,'' in M. Schreiber (ed), *Social Work and Mental Retardation*, New York: John Day.

C.M. Parkes (1975), *Bereavement: Studies of Grief in Adult Life*, Penguin.

Video

Helping the Mentally Handicapped and their Families (1984) Videotext Educational Publishing/University of Exeter.

7

What do parents want from social workers?

R ecently a colleague told me that she had visited a family whose 17 year old daughter was manifesting a number of behavioural problems. Although the young woman would be leaving school within two years the family had received no contact at all from social services. "My immediate feeling", the social worker recalled, "was that I should have been here 17 years ago!"

Owens and Birchenall (1979) interviewed social workers from various local authorities and concluded that in terms of their current role of working with mentally handicapped people and their families, "the majority felt their involvement was minimal ... There was felt to be a lack of liaison with other agencies. The priorities issue came in for much criticism".

While it would be pathologising families with a mentally handicapped member to insist they have a social worker, "community care" is not a reality without specialist support. As Owens and Birchenall point out: "For the past decade, much emphasis has been placed on community care, but often the fact has been minimised that its basis is the family, with the burden of care falling very heavily on the largest unpaid section of society; that is the mother".

In most studies parents record a lack of contact with social services unless they meet with a crisis, when they tend to be treated as "a problem"

Table 7 *Family Fund mothers contact with social services*

Regularly	10.9%
4 months to 1 year	13.9%
Occasionally i.e. for specific things	60.49
Never	12.5%
Don't know/remember	2.3%

(*from Philip and Duckworth, 1982*)

Other problems experienced were:

☐ Not knowing what social services were meant to provide.
☐ Fear that social services were agents of social control rather than advice and assistance.
☐ Social workers' lack of specialist knowledge.
☐ The high turnover in staff.

☐ Red tape and delays in the provision of services.

A local survey of all parents with a mentally handicapped child or adult living at home in the district of Mid Sussex (population 114,000) found that parents had to approach many different sources to find reliable information, often finding other parents the most informative. Many services which should have been well publicised were not known by every family.

Table 8 *Families with children: Knowledge of resources*

	Heard of	Used (a percentage of those who were aware of the service)
Aids and adaptations	55%	29%
Special nappies and incontinence pads	66%	68%
Attendance Allowance	89%	74%
Wheelchairs	68%	38%
Mobility Allowance	76%	41%
Toy library	74%	46%

For the adult group, 30 per cent had never heard of Attendance Allowance, only 43 per cent knew about provisions for respite care, and only 22 per cent were aware of the local authority's ability to provide aids and adaptations in the home (Elfield and Gilbert, 1980).

Social workers sometimes appear confused as to how to approach parents when they seem to get contradictory messages:

"I think the biggest help you can give us is first to sit and let us talk" (quoted in Glendinning, 1983).

"It's no good, sympathy without action" (quoted in Hanvey, 1981).

In fact there is no dichotomy: families want both a good listener and someone who turns what he hears into practical action.

Parents would like social workers to meet them at least half way:

"The initiative should always come from the social worker".

"They never come to you, you always have to hammer on their door!"

Social workers should be knowledgeable themselves and know where to unearth what they don't know at the time:

"All social workers should equip themselves with more knowledge of mentally handicapped children to enable *sound* advice to be given" (Elfield and Gilbert, 1980).

Although many remarks in the published surveys are critical, parents have expressed satisfaction when social workers have offered:

- ☐ *Regular support, time and comfort*, where the professional visitor can alleviate the isolation that many parents suffer from. This is only beneficial, however, when coupled with
- ☐ *Practical information and practical assistance.* Parents need to feel that the social worker is aware of the specific difficulties involved and of ways of meeting a variety of needs. Sometimes help with a financial benefit, information on where to get incontinence aids, advice on holiday schemes etc. may alleviate a great deal of anxiety.
- ☐ *Specialist knowledge.* The social worker should know the individual child and have some basic knowledge of his or her intrinsic condition.
- ☐ *Contact with other people in similar situations*, for the sharing of common problems and the pooling of information.
- ☐ *Contact with social services at specific times*, to identify current needs and anticipate future ones.
- ☐ *Co-ordination with other agencies*, such as education and health.
- ☐ *Access to respite care*, to give parents time to themselves and the other children in the family, in a form that is not guilt-inducing.
- ☐ *The development of varied provision*, to meet individual needs and aid individual development.
- ☐ *Safeguards for future care*, to reduce anxiety and promote healthy independence.

"What is needed for our sons and daughters", wrote one respondent to our survey, "is permanent residential care with daily attendance in an adult training centre or sheltered workshop to get settled into, before we die. This is the worry of all parents who are elderly. Hospital or institutional care is not acceptable, *the mentally handicapped man or woman needs privacy and dignity*".

- ☐ *Developmental programmes*, such as portage or the Haringey "FISH" Project, which involves social workers, using a behavioural approach to work specifically with the problems of having a mentally handicapped person in the family (Kiernan, 1982).
- ☐ *Partnership.* Although parents must be allowed to be parents and not some kind of pseudo-professional, they are experts in their own right, and the principles of partnership should always be observed:
  - Mutual respect and recognition of the essential equality between parents and professionals.
  - The sharing of information and skills.
  - Sharing of feelings.
  - Sharing the process of decision-making.
  - Recognition of the individuality of families and the uniqueness of the handicapped person.

As Glendinning concluded in her 1983 survey: "The parents in this study felt that, on the whole, their needs were being overlooked in the current ethos and organisation of statutory welfare services. In essence, what they advocated was a greater emphasis on routine support and the prevention of, rather than reaction to, crises".

Reading

C. Glendinning (1983), *Unshared Care: Parents and Their Disabled Children*, Chapter 7, Routledge & Kegan Paul.

C. Hanvey (1981), *Social Work with Mentally Handicapped People*, Chapter 2 Heinemann Educational/*Community Care*.

M. Philip and D. Duckworth (1982), *Children with Disabilities and Their Families: A Review of Research*, NFER-Nelson.

C. Hannam (1975), *Parents and Mentally Handicapped Children*, Chapters 4 and 8, Penguin/MIND.

D. Thomas (1982), *The Experience of Handicap*, Chapter 10, Methuen.

D. Anderson (1982), *Social Work and Mental Handicap*, Chapter 3, Macmillan.

P. Mittler and H. McConachie (ed) (1983), *Parents, Professionals and Mentally Handicapped People: Approaches to Partnership*, Croom Helm.

C. Kiernan (1982), *Family Involvement with Services in Haringay*, Thomas Coram Research Unit.

G. Owens and P. Birchenall (1979), *Mental Handicap: The Social Dimensions*, Pitman Medical.

P. Beresford and S. Croft, "Living Together: A Redefinition of Group Care Services", in T. Philpot (ed) (1984), *Group Care Practice*, *Community Care*/Business Press International.

M. Elfield and P. Gilbert (1980), *Report on the Questionnaire Sent to Parents of Mentally Handicapped Persons in the Mid Sussex Area.* Unpublished.

8

The role of the social worker

Social work with mentally handicapped people and their families can properly be seen as beginning with the 1913 Mental Deficiency Act which laid down that local authorities should be responsible for:

- ☐ The ascertainment of mentally handicapped people.
- ☐ The provision and maintenance of suitable institutions.
- ☐ The care, through appointed officers, of "mental defectives" in the community: including the conveyance of patients to and from institutions; the overall care of cases under guardianship; and the supervision of those for whom statutory care was deemed unnecessary.

These duties were sometimes undertaken directly by the local authority, sometimes by voluntary workers, and were the starting point of a counselling service to families. The guardianship provisions were used flexibly to provide parents with financial help or to enable those without relatives, in one of the institutions, to be placed with a family.

In terms of residential care there were about 2,000 "mentally defective patients" in 1914 receiving "treatment" in institutions built in the middle of the 19th century or under the 1886 Idiots Act. The largest of these were the five original hospitals for "idiots", such as the Royal Earlswood near Redhill, Surrey. In addition there were unspecified numbers of mentally handicapped people in the workhouses, county asylums or private establishments. From 1913, local authorities built small and then larger "colonies" until 2,000 bed institutions were drawing inmates from large catchment areas, effectively severing parental contact.

Day care was a later development, training centres for both children and adults appearing first on a voluntary basis, being built up gradually by local authorities, taken over the the newly formed NHS in 1948 and returned to the local authority (education and social services) in 1971.

As a number of psychiatric social workers (PSWs) entered the field, the number of trained staff increased, but studies showed a low priority given to mentally handicapped people and their families despite the creation of a unified mental health service in 1948. In 1959 the Younghusband report made a clear statement about social work orientation:

"We regard the essential functions of social workers in the health and welfare services as being to assess the disturbance of equilibrium in a given handicapped person and his family and social relationships so as to give appropriate help. The aim will be to offer a supporting relationship in which his and their fears, frustrations and anxieties are understood, and measures used to meet or lessen them, and also to further a better personal and social adjustment and a renewed ability to exercise responsibility by whatever means are indicated for a given person at a given time'' (HMSO (1959), *Report of the Working Party on Social Workers in the Local Authority and Welfare Services*).

At the same time the 1959 Mental Health Act confirmed the position of the mental welfare officer (MWO) (see figure 13) and obliged local authorities to provide for care and after-care in the case of persons suffering from mental disorders. The 1959 Act also abolished the requirement for social workers' visits that had been bitterly resented by some families, but meant that many now had no support at all. Michael Bayley's well-known survey in Sheffield in the 1970s found that only 44 per cent of the severely mentally handicapped adults living at home were visited by an MWO. The social workers were also hampered by lack of clear guidelines and adequate community resources. As Bayley (1973) stated: ''There appeared to be a general uncertainty among the mental welfare officers about the sort of service they should be trying to offer to the mentally subnormal and their families, let alone how to offer it''.

The year 1971 saw the implementation of the Seebohm report in the creation of unified social services departments and the publication of the government White Paper, *Better Services for the Mentally Handicapped*. Both supported and strengthened the role of the social worker. Seebohm stated: ''The families of mentally disordered people tend to suffer from inter-related social disabilities . . . the social workers should be concerned with the whole family . . . to make a family diagnosis . . . to take wide responsibility . . . and mobilise a wide range of resources'' (HMSO (1968) *Report of the Committee on Local Authority and Allied Personal Social Services*, CMND 3703).

The new departments should have brought new resources and a wider perspective and range of skills to the service of mentally handicapped people and their families. Instead there was a return to the pre-1959 ideology of this client group not requiring trained workers, and Goldberg *et al*, (1978) showed them receiving a very low priority. Many opportunities have been missed since 1971, for as Shearer pointed out: ''It is social workers, after all, who have the perspective of the whole family rather than the child in isolation; and it is they who are geared to lengthy patient support through changing family needs, rather than to occasional and limited interventions to meet a specific need'' (A. Shearer (1978), ''The Barnardo's Chorley Project'', *Social Work Today*, Vol 10. No. 7).

On the margins of society

It is sometimes difficult to define exactly what social work is and it is often therefore reduced to a catalogue of duties carried out by statute. Two of the essential elements in social work, however, which are especially vital to its

Figure 13 *The evolution of the approved social worker*

Date	Case worker	Authorised officer
1834 Poor Law Act		Poor law relieving officer
1913 Mental Deficiency Act	Mental deficiency visitor	Poor law relieving officer, some acting as "specially authorised officer"
1929 Local Government Act and 1930 Mental Treatment Act	Mental deficiency visitors and psychiatric social workers	Public assistance officers acting as "duly authorised officers"
1948 Implementation of National Health Service Act	Mental health social workers	As above
1954 Formation of Society of Mental Welfare Officers	"Mental welfare officers"	
1959 Mental Health Act	Mental welfare officers (created by statute)	
1971 Implementation of Local Authority Social Services Act	Social workers	Social workers (operating as MWOs for the purposes of the 1959 Act)
1974 National Health Service Re-organisation	Hospital social workers became part of social services	
1983 Mental Health Act	Approved social workers Generic and specialist social workers	

expression, are work with people who are experiencing situations involving loss and change, and with those who are in conflict with the norms and expectations of the society in which they live (see Anderson, 1982).

People with a mental handicap may transgress norms by their behaviour or even by their very existence, as many parents have found to their cost: "Some round here seem to think it's like leprosy and they or their kids might catch it, so they steer clear. There's an attitude that you can't be quite right if you've produced a handicapped child". (quoted in McCormack, 1978).

Having a dependant with a mental handicap within the family may cause isolation within the family itself, within the neighbourhood and kinship network, or even a splitting-off from one's fundamental beliefs. As one Methodist minister has written: "The tragedy was not so much Arthur as my sense of abandonment, my inability to accept the existence and love of God at those deeper levels where it makes a real difference to one's life" (Young, 1985).

Frances Young found love, acceptance and support from her church community, "a community without barriers, where all kinds of odd bits of humanity can find they have a place." Society does not often provide that kind of acceptance, however, and social workers, who have always been at the leading-edge of experience, where barriers are erected and dismantled, have to be marginal people, patrolling the boundaries and enclosures, the fens and the streets, to build bridges, gates and fords where none existed before or where they had gone to ruin.

In practical terms this may mean a paediatric social worker helping medical and nursing staff come to terms with their feelings about loss and imperfection, and setting-up better ways to counsel parents. It could mean a social worker ensuring that facilities for the under-fives are open to handicapped children. Social work has to respond to the spirit of integration in the 1981 Education Act. Protecting the interests of mentally handicapped people interviewed by the police (see chapter 13), and increasing the opportunities for ordinary employment and leisure facilities are all places where the social worker can gradually expand the normative concepts of society and protect the interests of vulnerable people. Martin Davies, in his book *The Essential Social Worker*, sees one of social work's prime tasks as "contributing to the maintenance and growth of those citizens seen to be deprived and underprivileged, and trying to enrich the lives of those on the margins of society" (Davies, 1981).

The role of the paediatric social worker

"There is no nice easy way", wrote parent, Mary McCormack, "of finding out that your child is mentally handicapped — only awful ways and slightly less awful ways" (McCormack, 1978).

The birth of a handicapped child is a crisis which threatens the integrity of the parents individually and as a partnership. The couple have to be supported through the crisis period and helped to undertake and progress through the griefwork, of emancipation from the bondage to loss; readjusting to the environment in which the loss is actualised; and formulating new coping strategies.

While the paediatrician has the responsibility to inform parents of their child's handicap and is in the best position to discuss causation and prognosis, the paediatric social worker should be able to give parents the emotional support and time to absorb the information they have received and listen for questions, hinted at or half-stated, that can be answered there and then or referred back to the paediatrician; for, as Mary McCormack has written, "It is not a case of not knowing the answers, but of not even knowing the questions" (McCormack, 1978).

Other duties in broad categories are:

☐ *Protecting the interests of the child* under the requirements of the 1969 Children and Young Persons Act. For example, in the "Alexandra" case of 1981, Hammersmith Social Services Department sought and obtained wardship for a baby with Down's Syndrome, after her parents had refused her a routine life-saving operation. "Alexandra" was fostered for a time and eventually returned to her parents (for a fuller discussion see BASW (1982), *Guidelines on Social Work with Severely Handicapped Infants*).

☐ *Counselling for other members of the family*:
   ● *grandparents*, who will also be undergoing a crisis and who may need help themselves to enable them to fulfil their supportive role with the parents.
   ● *siblings*, who could suffer from neglect, displacement, guilt, anxiety and so on.

☐ *Support for hospital staff*, who often find that the birth of a handicapped child strikes at their professional integrity as "curers". The social worker should keep staff informed of new developments in community care so that realistic advice can be given and decisions taken.

☐ *Liaising with community services* to ensure that support continues and appropriate domiciliary services are provided once hospital care diminishes.

The role of the social worker in the multi-disciplinary team

The Court report of 1976 recommended that the division between health and social services could best be healed by the creation of "district handicap teams" (DHTs). The National Development Group pamphlet of the following year stated that " ... families themselves are the first and best resource a child can have ... support can best be developed by the operation of a multi-disciplinary community mental handicap team drawing its personnel from both the NHS and local authorities" (NDG (1977), *Mentally Handicapped Children: A Plan for Action*).

The Court report's idea was for the DHT to work with *all* handicapped children up till about 16 years and then hand over responsibility for those with a mental handicap to the community mental handicap team (CMHT). Recent research has, however, shown little consistency in operation throughout England (M. Plank (1982), *Teams for Mentally Handicapped People*, Campaign for Mentally Handicapped People). In fact 50 per cent of the CMHTs in the survey worked with both children and adults. While this may present some philosophical difficulties it does provide a very consistent approach and avoids a complete change of personnel in adolescence.

The aim of the CMHT is not to replace the generic workers. Its function is to supplement them in such a way as to bridge the gaps that often exist between agencies, especially for instance at school-leaving age; to provide a specialist service to those who have special needs, for example those persons with additional physical, sensory or psychiatric impairments which require very strong co-ordination between health and social services; to develop procedures for the comprehensive assessment of individual needs; and to aid joint planning (see National Development Team (1976/7), *First Report*).

Membership of the CMHT will vary widely due to local circumstances. The NDG pamphlet No. 2 suggests that the community mental handicap nurse (CMHN) and specialist social worker will be the core members, backed up by other professionals such as clinical psychologist, consultant in mental handicap, specialist health visitor, and occupational, physio- and speech therapists. The Campaign for Mentally Handicapped People survey showed that approximately 80 per cent of the survey teams had a community nurse and social worker but very few had therapists. Probably only relatively well-funded districts will have a wide team membership (eg see *Operational Policy* for the CMHTs, Wandsworth District Health Authority, June 1983).

In the kind of CMHT outlined by Simon (1981) the roles of team members should be complementary. As probably the only local authority representative in a multi-disciplinary team, the social worker has a vital liaising function. Simon says: "He represents the link between families in their homes, the wider community and the services which should be available within that community through social services and voluntary agencies".

Although many of the tasks will overlap among the team members the social worker's special expertise should give him the following roles:

☐ *Social biographer*. To enable the family look at needs and the team to offer appropriate help a full social history/assessment must be compiled. This helps place the individual within the family unit and the family into a wider kinship and community context (see figures 14 and 18). A good assessment in the initial stages can avoid misunderstandings and prevent the parents having to repeat intimate and heart-searing details to every team member. As the team's work is partnership, parents should be offered the opportunity to have a copy of the report.

☐ *Link person* to provide a link between families and community services and between the various agencies (see figure 20).

☐ *Knowledge of benefits and resources.* Families who have coped in adversity for many years often feel defeated by the lack of some form of practical assistance during a crisis period. The social worker should have a good working knowledge of financial benefits, domiciliary help and resources.

☐ *Counsellor.* The social worker should have a great deal to offer as a personal counsellor to mentally handicapped persons and any member of the family who is experiencing the pain of the situation.

☐ *Co-ordinator.* Arrange assessment, short-term care, respite care and day care in social service facilities, leading on from a comprehensive multi-disciplinary assessment in the home.

☐ *Knowledge base.* Collate and disseminate specialist knowledge on resources and other matters to colleagues in area teams.

☐ *Initiator and/or supporter of groups.* As the 1971 White Paper states: "Many parents obtain relief and reassurance from contact with other parents of mentally handicapped children". Social workers should be a point of contact for families, especially those newly arrived in an area, so that support groups can be set up and maintained, serving a variety of needs: parents, siblings and the extended family.

☐ *Educator.* The social work member of the team has a vital role in not only disseminating information and liaising between health and social services but also promoting exchange placements for staff to foster better understanding and personal links.

☐ *Planner.* Planning should start with the consumer, and the social worker being in direct contact with individuals, families and groups, is in a good position to identify gaps in the service and bring these to the attention of the management.

Simon warns that "in newly developing team services, where the role of each member is evolving, there may be some inter-disciplinary rivalry". Traditionally the "rivalry" has been seen to focus on the community nurse (CMHN) and social worker, as effectively illustrated in Elliott-Cannon's paper in 1981 (C. Elliott-Cannon, "Do the Mentally Handicapped Need Specialist Community Nursing Care?", *Nursing Times*, 1 July 1981). In fact, however, the inter-disciplinary clash could as easily be between consultants in mental handicap and clinical psychologists, as learning theory becomes more important than medical science in working with people who have a "learning difficulty" (see A. Tyne, *Who's Consulted?*, CMH Enquiry Paper No 8), or between the psychologist and community nurse who have a role in teaching new skills and lessening anti-social behaviour.

Figure 14 *Outline for the social assessment report*

Name and Date of Birth:

Address:

Diagnosis:

Referrer:

Reason for Referral:

Family Structure:

Relationship	Name	Occupation	Address

Home circumstances: *Space and amenities*   *Financial Constraints*

Family history:

Subject's history:

Family relationships: *Within immediate and extended family*

Social contacts and   *Neighbours, friends, church, clubs etc.*
  relationships:

Agency contacts: *G.P., Health Visitor, voluntary society, consultant etc.*

Benefits: *Attendance Allowance, Mobility Allowance etc.*

Assessments: *Psychometric and Skills*

Subject's current   *Playgroup, school, training centre, employment etc.*
  occupation:

Leisure interests:

Health: *Including medication*

Current concerns:

Conclusion: *Including action to be undertaken*

In their formation stage multi-disciplinary teams should be looking at the general needs of persons with a mental handicap, and the specific objectives for service provision as identified in their area. If team members can then be honest about their limitations as well as their skills, and if a keyworker system is implemented (as in 71 per cent of the CMH survey teams) then an overlap of roles will be complementary rather than a cause of conflict.

Figure 15 *The role of the community nurse and clinical psychologist*

CMHN	Clinical psychologist
1 To collect a baseline history and information on the level of functioning and competence of the individual.	1 Assessment of cognitive ability, personality, and skills of individuals.
2 To plan and implement behavioural and skills programmes.	2 Precision teaching of skills to individuals.
3 To provide a link with community services.	3 Assessment and amelioration of behavioural problems.
4 To provide practical help and advice to families.	4 Act as a consultant on learning and behaviour to other team members.
5 To provide nursing care when needed and to monitor the client's treatment with regard to medication for epilepsy etc.	5 Provision of advice and training to other agencies.
6 Offer a follow-up service to mentally handicapped people discharged from hospital.	

Working with colleagues

As Angelo Roncalli once wrote about a different set of changing circumstances: "The past will never return. New situations require new dispositions". Longing for a return to the days of the mental welfare officer is not productive, but there is a profound challenge to any new system of service delivery to meet the difficult task of reconciling families' needs for planned contact over many years and knowledgeable input when specific problems arise; and also the needs of specialist agencies for contact with a recognised social worker.

With the appointment of increasing numbers of specialist social workers

Figure 16: *The needs of mentally handicapped people and their families and the help required in meeting them*

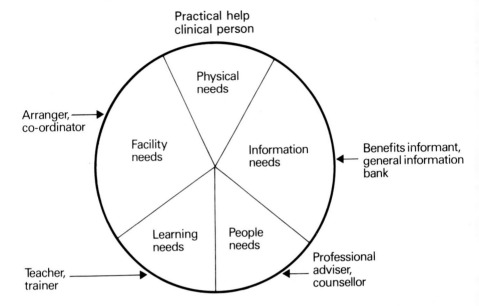

to multi-disciplinary teams over recent years there is the danger of a divide opening between generic and specialist social workers. Unless there is a sensible division of roles the specialists may be seen merely as creating more work for their colleagues in area or patch teams.

Figure 17: *Complementary roles within the CMHT*

Needs	Information	Facilities	People	Learning	Physical
Skills	Collating/communicating	Co-ordinating	Counselling	Training	Clinical
Worker	SW/CMHN	SW/CMHN	All disciplines	CMHN/Psychologists (SW?)	CMHN/consultant in mental handicap

Specialist workers should be able to work effectively in the area of assessment, and with families and individuals to surmount developmental crises. They should also be able to set up liaison and monitoring schemes so as to defuse the potential for the traumatic crises which often arise from poor service design and delivery.

Inevitably some clients will require more longer term support than a small specialist team can give. Effective communication and co-operation with

Figure 18: *Sociograph of network support. Such a diagram may assist families, social workers and colleagues to look at kinship and professional support, perceive gaps or overlap, and adjust the situation accordingly*

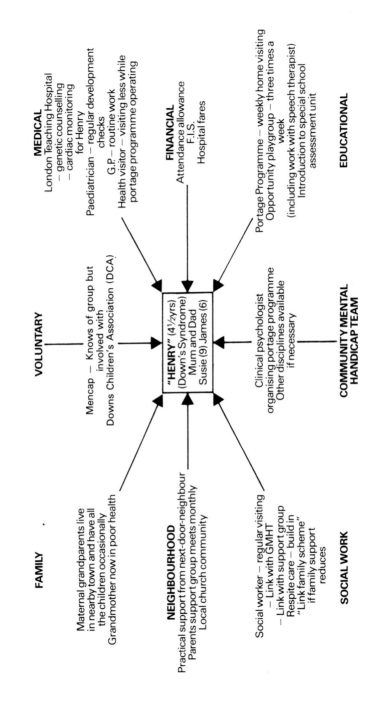

MEDICAL
London Teaching Hospital
– genetic counselling
– cardiac monitoring
for Henry
Paediatrician – regular development checks
G.P. – routine work
Health visitor – visiting less while portage programme operating

FINANCIAL
Attendance allowance
F.I.S.
Hospital fares

EDUCATIONAL
Portage Programme – weekly home visiting
Opportunity playgroup – three times a week
(including work with speech therapist)
Introduction to special school assessment unit

VOLUNTARY
Mencap – Knows of group but involved with Downs Children's Association (DCA).

"HENRY" (4½yrs)
(Down's Syndrome)
Mum and Dad
Susie (9) James (6)

COMMUNITY MENTAL HANDICAP TEAM
Clinical psychologist organising portage programme
Other disciplines available if necessary

FAMILY
Maternal grandparents live in nearby town and have all the children occasionally
Grandmother now in poor health

NEIGHBOURHOOD
Practical support from next-door-neighbour
Parents support group meets monthly
Local church community

SOCIAL WORK
Social worker – regular visiting
– Link with GMHT
– Link with support group
Respite care – build in
"Link family scheme" if family support reduces

69

Figure 19 *Planned contact with families (children and young adults)*

Age	Liaison with other agencies
notification of handicap	Paediatric services in hospital and community
2 years	Child assessment services Playgroup
9 years	Child health School
13 years	Education service (in line with the 1981 Education Act's assessment) Respite services, if used
18 years	School or further education centre ATC/SEC Education counsellor Careers service
21 years	Career service ATC/SEC Residential centre

area colleagues is therefore essential and it may help if each generic team has a designated social worker or assistant to do long term work following specialist assessment.

The role of the social worker in the mental handicap hospital

The siting of most mental hospitals and their position in the medical priority list following the creation of the NHS left them "isolated, not only geographically and socially, but also from the mainstream of both medical and educational advances" (P. Morris (1969), *Put Away*, Routledge & Kegan Paul).

Although it was recognised as far back as the 1926 Royal Commission that mental institutions needed a "go-between" with the wider community, because "the transition from asylum life to the everyday world is a stage of peculiar difficulty", very few social workers were appointed. This was partly due to the unpopularity of the work with PSWs and the fact that until 1974 the appointment of social workers was at the discretion of hospital managers. Following the 1959 Mental Health Act, mental welfare officers were appointed (Section 8) to supervise "mentally disordered persons of any description", including those in hospital. Pauline Morris's survey of institutions for mentally handicapped people recorded a low standard of training in hospital social workers and little interest from the MWOs employed by the local authority. Kathleen Jones' later study (K. Jones, 1975) also showed a low priority given to recruiting social work staff in mental handicap hospitals. The National Development Group's 1978 report, *Helping Mentally Handicapped People in Hospital* was positive in its opinion: "We fail to understand how any mental handicap hospital can be capable of functioning effectively without any social work input ... within the hospital the social worker should take a full part in the multi-disciplinary team work necessary for the proper functioning of the hospital" (Section 7.6).

The social worker has a major role in the following areas:

- [ ] *Interpreting the individual and family to hospital staff* so that barriers are not erected which might sever contact between the resident and his family. A social history compiled for this purpose will ensure that the person's past is preserved even if family links are broken by time and bereavement.
- [ ] *Interpreting the hospital to the individual and his family* Although hospitals are much more open than in the past, any institution is daunting to those outside it. Being employed by an agency outside the NHS, the social worker is able to facilitate communication.
- [ ] *Liaising between the hospital and outside agencies*, especially the local social services offices, hostels and training centres with whom good contact is needed and who may be able to provide specialist workers, volunteers, training facilities etc.
- [ ] *Aiding the rehabilitation of residents* by sharing in multi-disciplinary conferences, investigating suitable placements, co-operating in rehabilitative training and supporting placements together with other rehabilitation staff.
- [ ] *Advice concerning residents' welfare rights* and also those of families who may find visiting difficult without financial help.
- [ ] *Liaising with parents*, together with the nursing staff, on any changes that may affect their relatives.
- [ ] *Undertaking statutory functions* in regard to children in hospital who are in the care of the local authority.
- [ ] *Liaison with area social work staff* in respect of statutory duties under the 1983 Mental Health Act, and in regard to children in the hospital who are in the care of the local authority or may need child care legislation to protect their rights.

The social worker in the resource centre

As interest in and commitment to work with mentally handicapped people and their families grows, it is likely that local authorities will have a number of alternatives for providing a domiciliary service to individuals and their families. Hostel or adult training centre/social education centre staff might provide both:

- [ ] A domiciliary service to families.
- [ ] Support for individuals living in a "core and cluster system" (see chapter 9).

The resource centre, be it a day or residential facility, could offer:

- [ ] Continuing assessment.

- [ ] Phased training for independence.
- [ ] A meeting place for parents and other support groups.
- [ ] Support, advice and re-training for individuals in substitute families or independent living situations.

Keeping in contact

If a fieldwork model is used while the mentally handicapped person is still with his family then support to families must be on a planned basis, not just as a reaction to crises, because as Glendinning (*Unshared Care*, Routledge and Kegan Paul, 1983) points out: "Many parents felt that a routine, regular visit from a social worker would help enormously. It would lend a sense of security... their current needs could be readily identified and future ones anticipated and planned for" (see figure 19).

A specialist "patch" system

The strategy of the specialist team should be to present the "human face" of the department by being a recognised contact person at places such as special schools, ATCs and voluntary groups where mentally handicapped people and their families are likely to congregate (see figure 20). Just as with community social work, this specialist "patch" system should give families and specialist agencies the kind of informal social work that many valued in the pre-Seebohm days, without the "tunnel vision" that was often prevalent in the old specialist departments.

A social worker from the specialist team should be in regular contact with all the specialist services in that particular area, in order to:
- [ ] Create confidence in social services by giving speedy access to social work time and by reinforcing goodwill in the belief that each party wishes to communicate.
- [ ] Give individuals and their families the opportunity to gain information or talk through difficulties without going through a formal referral procedure.
- [ ] Facilitate contact and mutual understanding between the various groups and resources.
- [ ] Facilitate the constructive transfer of individuals from one setting to another — for example, when leaving a special school.
- [ ] Collate needs that will have to be met by policy changes and inter-agency co-operation.
- [ ] Present a consistent and familiar face to clients, families and staff from many disciplines.

If such a strategy is used then agencies and families will gain more confidence in social workers and knowledge of what they can offer.

The specialist worker may be able to meet the parents of a handicapped child shortly after the diagnosis is made and work with them through that first traumatic period. Long-term work may not be seen as appropriate, especially by the family themselves who may not want to be seen as needing a social worker purely because they have a handicapped child. The specialist should make it clear that she can be contacted again at any time and the use of a social services information handbook (for example, P. Gilbert and J. Hollingdale, 1985) is helpful as something to reinforce the offer.

Figure 20: *Liaison strategy for a specialist team*

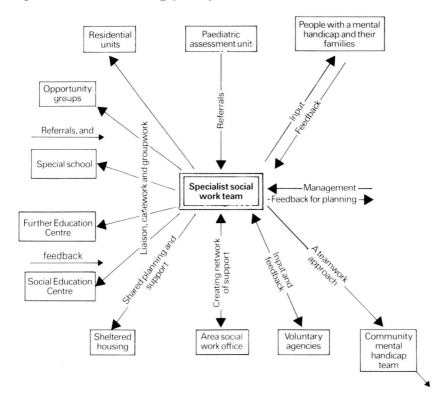

The social worker can thus initiate contact with the family at future possible crisis points and facilitate entry to playgroup; the transfer from playgroup to school; undertake assessments under the 1981 Education Act with good knowledge of both the child and resources; co-ordinate plans at the school-leaving stage; give relevant information on benefits and resources at crucial ages; and draw parents with similar needs together to share worries and strategies for coping.

The consumer's voice

"Mentally handicapped people everywhere," write Paul Williams and Bonnie Shoultz, "are beginning to have a voice of their own" (*We can Speak for Ourselves*, Souvenir Press, 1982). While the need to involve parents in decision-making has only recently been recognised, the need to involve mentally handicapped people themselves remains in its infancy.

Although casework is not easy with a person who may have impaired

73

intelligence or poor communication skills it should be attempted (see Symington, 1981). If the traditional approach is not possible then it is vital that the worker develop means of dialogue through signing, pictures, video etc, to enable the client communicate his world views, hopes, wishes and fears (see figure 21).

Figure 21:   *The use of Kinetic family drawings*

Figure 21 is the kinetic family drawing (see Burns and Kaufman, 1971) done by a twenty year old woman, "Norma", who had a mild intellectual handicap and a very claustrophobic family. "Norma" was admitted to residential care for assessment following outbursts of aggression towards her mother. On admittance "Norma" was very withdrawn and she was encouraged to draw her feelings and her situation as she saw it. "Norma's" picture tells us a number of things apart from the very obvious phallic symbols revealing her sexual frustration, which vented itself in a desperate desire for sexual expression when she was released from the confines of home. The shaded areas above and below are characteristic of people from unstable families; the position of the father denotes his lack of status within the family group, especially in relation to "Mrs. Thomas" who interposes between him and "Norma"; the watering cans are not only phallic but also symbols of aggression and struggles for power and independence; the house is menacing and prison-like with its small windows and the facial imagery in the door.

Groupwork can be immensely useful in helping those with difficulties in learning to develop both as individuals and as members of a social group. Many mentally handicapped people are at the very early developmental stage of finding it difficult to separate from their parents and take on an identity of their own. Skilled groupwork can encourage positive concepts of self and others; increase awareness of identity and needs; draw out feelings long locked away; and develop a sense of greater responsibility through the articulation of desires and choices. Verbal communication is not always necessary; mime, drawing etc. can be just as illuminating if the worker is imaginative.

The needs of the family and the mentally handicapped individual are often in a delicate balance, and, for instance, when arranging respite care for families, it is important that the rights of the individual to self-determination are not overlooked. As was discussed in chapter 5, times of loss and change can be even more traumatic for someone with a mental handicap; the loss of a parent or the closure of a residential home often means the uprooting of an individual from a community with many friendship ties. Imaginative provision can be sensitive to the consumer's voice and preserve the vital links in the chain of friendship, acceptance and support. Getting the focus right is at its most important on those rare occasions when the shock of handicap for a parent places the child at risk. This was tragically demonstrated in May, 1984 when Louise Brown, an infant with Down's Syndrome, was killed by her father.

Training

Two documents stress the need for better training to develop a more sensitive and professional approach: CCETSW (1974), *People with Handicaps Need Better Trained Workers* and MIND's 1977 document *The Mental Handicap Component in Social Work Training*. Government reports, professional groups and parent bodies have urged social workers to develop their role in this field.

Conclusion

In one of the most recent research studies of families with a severely disabled child, social services' low profile with this client group was starkly demonstrated: 39 per cent did not know the location of their local social services department; 51 per cent could not name a social worker whom they would ask to see; and 35 per cent could not name even one kind of help available from social services (Glendinning, 1984).

The parents in the survey very much valued the caring and informal support they received from the specialist workers. Sixty eight per cent considered "counselling" — the discussion of feelings and anxieties about the disabled child — to be of very great value, while 56 per cent identified the feeling of support they derived from having someone to turn to if needed to be the "single most valuable feature" of their contact with the specialist social worker: "It was like having a friend I could lean on, who could put me in touch with anyone who could help me. She seemed to be able to advise me on any problem. She had a lot of experience".

The next most frequently mentioned help was the information and practical help which contact with the worker had brought, especially that much of it had been spontaneous: "She found out about everything, whereas the social services don't — if you ask them about one problem they will find out about that but that's all, they never give you any other information". When asked by the research follow-up whether they would have preffered the cost of the service to be given in the form of a cash allowance instead most replied that money could not replace a personal service.

The challenge of mental handicap; its effect on the individual, his family and environment over a long period; the exercise of specialist knowledge while keeping in contact with good generic practice; the need for personal care, imaginative and careful listening, practical information and support; and the requirement for effective co-ordination between agencies — these demand a social work service every bit as skilled as in child care.

A social work service will have to be imaginative to combine the task-centred and long-term supportive elements needed in this area of work in a comprehensive system. Social work must become local, visible, capable and flexible so that families and agencies can begin to trust a service which becomes both accessible and dependable. Only in a radical assessment of priorities and a new orientation can social work take its part as the 1971 White Paper envisaged: "The person best placed to act as a co-ordinator is likely to be the social worker, who should take her part in the multi-disciplinary team as soon as handicap is suspected and thereafter maintain a continuing relationship with a handicapped child and his family."

Reading
C. Hanvey (1981), *Social Work with Mentally Handicapped People*, Heinemann Educational/*Community Care*.
D. Anderson (1982), *Social Work and Mental Handicap*, Macmillan.
E. Browne (1982), *Mental Handicap: The Role for Social Workers*, Sheffield University/*Community Care*.
K. Jones (1972), *A History of the Mental Health Services*, Routledge and Kegan Paul.
K. Jones (1975), *Opening the Door*, Routledge & Kegan Paul.
M. McCormack (1978), *A Mentally Handicapped Child in the Family*, Constable.
G. Simon (ed) (1981), *Local Services for Mentally Handicapped People*, British Institute for Mental Handicap.
M. Bayley (1973), *Mental Handicap and Community Care*, Routledge and Kegan Paul.
P. Gilbert and B. Spooner, "Strength in Unity", *Community Care*, 28 October 1982.
P. Gilbert, "New Services, New Strategies", *Community Care*, 21 March 1983.
M. Goldberg *et al* (1978), "Towards Accountability in Social Work", *British Journal of Social Work*, Vol. 8 No. 3.
H. Prins, "The Contribution of Social Work to the Treatment of the

Mentally Disordered'', in R. Olsen (ed) (1976), *Differential Approaches in Social Work with the Mentally Disordered*, BASW.

P. Gilbert & J. Hollingdale (1985), *Coping with Mental Handicap in Horsham, Crawley and Mid Sussex*. West Sussex County Council.

N. Symington (1981), ''The Psychotherapy of a Subnormal Patient'', *British Journal of Medical Psychology*, No. 54.

C. Glendinning (1984), ''The Resource Worker Project: Evaluating a Specialist Social Work Service for Severely Disabled Children and Their Families'', *British Journal of Social Work*, Vol. 14 No. 2.

M. Davies (1981), *The Essential Social Worker*, Heinemann Educational/ Community Care.

F. Young (1985), *Face to Face*, Epworth Press.

T. Ryan & R. Walker (1985), *Making Life Story Books*, British Agencies for Adoption and Fostering.

H. England (due for publication 1986), *Social Work as Art: Making Sense for Good Practice*, Allen & Unwin.

9

Principles of service delivery

S ervice delivery hinges almost entirely on the nature of the prevailing philosophy. As we have seen from chapter 3, this has in effect meant service patterns derived from a view of mentally handicapped people as being either a threat to society or in danger from it.

The developmental philosophy that manifested itself in the 19th century, and again in the 1970s, sees mentally handicapped people as capable of developing skills and intrinsically worthy of citizenship. The prevailing philosophy in government and professional circles in the United Kingdom is that of "normalisation", which was first defined by Wolfensberger, and expressed since as: "Letting the mentally retarded obtain an existence as close to normal as possible" (Bank-Mikkelson); and "Making available to the mentally handicapped patterns and conditions of everyday life which are as close as possible to the norms and patterns of the mainstream of society" (Nirje).

The normalisation principle argues for a reversal of past policies and their replacement by services which give a cultural value to mentally handicapped people. Thus philosophy shapes services which in turn influence images and concepts.

Figure 22 *From stigma to value*

Past policies	Normalisation principle
Dehumanisation	Enhancing dignity and individual respect through: individualisation, developing choice, value-giving language and images, and participation
Keeping individuals as children	Making activities appropriate to the age of the individual
Segregation	Integration through the localisation of services and public education

There are two main dangers in this philosophy: first, the danger of any philosophy, that it will degenerate into a narrow ideology; and, second, normalisation may "mean much greater pressure on mentally handicapped people to adjust to prevailing customs and standards" (Ryan and Thomas, 1980).

At its best "normalisation" means a restoration of the rights of citizenship; if distorted by those seeking merely to cut costs, it can lead to former hospital residents living in coastal boarding houses with no employment.

There are a number of publications outlining some of the projects which have taken place over the past decade:

A. Shearer, *A Community Service for Mentally Handicapped Children*, Barnardo Paper 4

V. Shennan (1983), *A Home of Their Own*, Souvenir Press

G. Jones and N. Tutt (eds) (1983), *A Way of Life for the Handicapped*, Social Care Association.

Tony Apolloni *et al* (ed) (1980), *Toward Excellence: Achievements in Residential Services for People with Disabilities*, University Park Press, Baltimore

The King's Fund has also produced two seminal project papers:

An Ordinary Life, Project Paper No. 24, 1982

An Ordinary Working Life, Project Paper, No. 50, 1984

Starting with the consumer

Service design should start with choice, with desire and desirability. There may be many conflicting needs and demands but these can be identified with practitioners then working out with individuals and their families how, perhaps competing desires can be reconciled. One method of translating perception into action is through Individual Programme Plans (IPPs).

The purpose of an IPP is to draw together the individual, his family, and those working with them to set clear and practical objectives over a time-

Figure 23:   *The individual programme planning cycle*

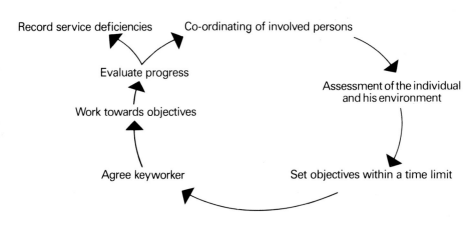

limited period (eg six months or a year). Several centres have developed such procedures. Among them are Mental Handicap in Wales — Applied Research Unit, The White House, 44/46 Cowbridge Road East, Cardiff, and the Health Care Evaluation Research Team, 45/47 Salisbury Road, The University, Highfield, Southampton.

IPPs are designed to start with an assessment of the individual's strengths, go on to a series of clearly defined objectives and set a date for evaluating them. The IPP should not be used to constrain a person's activities but rather to increase his horizons; it is not a way of justifying inadequate or invalid services, as a good IPP format will record deficiencies in the service which retard the individual's progress.

Evaluation of service systems

With assessment of the abilities of individuals increasingly popular it is only reasonable to see the development of a number of assessments of how services adequately relate to needs. Two examples are: The STAMINA checklists available from Mencap; and The PASS (Programme Analysis of Service Systems) set out in W. Wolfensberger and L. Glenn (1975), *Programme Analysis of Service Systems*, National Institute of Mental Retardation, Toronto. Campaign for Mentally Handicapped People (CMHP) run a series of workshops on PASS.

Service principles

In general the following principles should be observed so that services
- [ ] affirm and enhance the *dignity*, *self-respect* and *individuality* of mentally handicapped persons and their direct carers;
- [ ] engage mentally handicapped persons and their direct carers in the *partnership* of the planning process;
- [ ] engage the local communities' acceptance to bring about *integration*;
- [ ] build in *flexibility* so as to respond to current individual needs and changing needs;
- [ ] ensure that services are *locally based* in natural communities;
- [ ] utilise *generic* services first but build in specialist services as necessary;
- [ ] *co-ordinate* the varied services necessary to give a *comprehensive* service;
- [ ] place the *consumer* at the centre of the service;
- [ ] base the service on patterns of *culturally valued* normality in everyday living; and
- [ ] recognise the *potential* of the individual and social group and provide opportunities for the realisation of that potential.

Service design

The above principles dictate that services should respond to anyone with a disability as a person first, with the disability being an added dimension.

Maureen Oswin's study of short term care, *They Keep Going Away*, relates how, if service providers see children with a mental handicap as merely a burden to their parents rather than children with needs in their own right, then the service will do more harm than good in terms of long-term emotional damage.

> "A cardinal rule must be that children are clients in their own right and they must be provided with a quality of residential care that meets their individual needs with compassion and with skills that are firmly based on normal child care principles".

Specialist children's homes can provide a good experience for both handicapped children and their families but only if they are local and create good links with the families served. Special fostering schemes are increasingly popular as a flexible and local alternative to residential care, but if social workers see their role as merely gift-bearers, linking families and withdrawing, then the relationship is left unsupported: neither a professional service nor neighbourly care.

A good domiciliary service will reduce the numbers of children receiving short term care because of "problems" and look at the positive aspect of increasing their range of experiences. Families and their networks should be strengthened, not undermined, by professional intervention.

Figure 24: *Options in supporting families*

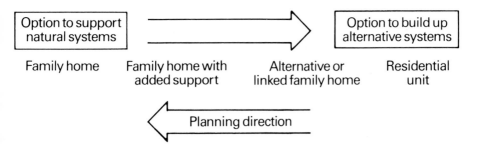

Continuity or continuum?

Many services are based on the concept of staff remaining static and clients subject to constant changes. New ideas in service design for living and working may see the development of "core and clusters" in both residential and day care. The advantages of the "cluster" system, based on a resource centre or administrative "core" is that, as a person becomes more or less dependent, he or she is not moved from one place to another, with its attendant anxiety, but given appropriate support from mobile staff.

Figure 25: *Example of a "core and cluster"*

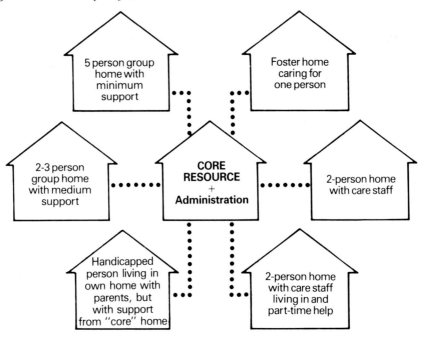

Employment options, even in a time of high unemployment, exist in various forms: independent work, job sharing, sheltered work eg sheltered industrial groups (SIGs), job attachment, supervised work, co-operatives and family businesses (examples in *An Ordinary Working Life*). There are many professionals with great experience in this field: careers officers, ATC staff, disablement resettlement officers (DROs), education counsellors etc, but the handover of responsibility from education to a plethora of services at school-leaving is still confusing, and the integration of people with disabilities needs to happen much earlier for a true vocational service to develop for adults.

In figure 9 (chapter 5) we saw the typical negative career pattern. This can be changed by a combination of creating opportunities for people with intellectual impairments and changing our attitude towards their worth and potential.

Integration or specialisation?

While the use of opportunity playgroups for young children keeps those with disabilities in the mainstream of life, and some local authorities are attempting to bring school age handicapped children onto the same campus as their peers in the spirit of the Warnock report and the 1981 Education

Figure 26: *Breaking into the vicious circle*

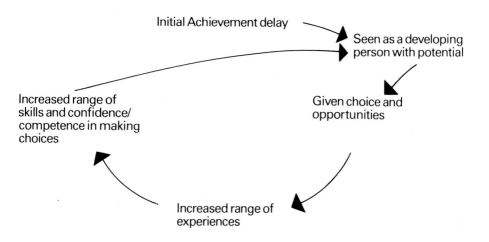

Act, attention is focusing on "mentally handicapped people with special problems", the title of a DHSS report in 1984.

The dilemma of service provision for mentally handicapped people with additional speech, visual or hearing impairments, behavioural disorders, and for those who reach old age, remains essentially the same as it did a century ago. As parents like Margaret Brock discovered, if you have an additional disability as well as an intellectual impairment the choice of resources is usually between the standard local service without the specialist help needed or a specialist facility many miles away from home and neighbourhood (Brock, 1984).

The 1984 DHSS study lists some of the factors which need to be taken into account when considering whether to provide a specialist facility:

For

- ☐ A specialist "back-up" service may give local facilities more confidence to accept more severely handicapped clients.
- ☐ Specialist units could provide respite for local homes and centres and return a "cured" client back to his home.
- ☐ Specialist staff will have special skills and the environment can be adapted to reduce difficulties, for example in the case of people with a severe visual impairment.
- ☐ The specialist unit can provide a "centre of excellence" to promote understanding and disseminate knowledge and skills.
- ☐ Specialist facilities can protect the interests of those with special needs *and* those less severely handicapped people who may receive less attention if staff time in the ordinary units is diverted to those with special needs.
- ☐ It may be easier to attract staff to designated specialist units.

- ☐ The availability of "back-up" units may encourage staff in ordinary units to give up too easily when faced with a difficult client and "pass the buck".
- ☐ Moving a handicapped person from one place to another may create more problems. Skills and behaviour learn in one setting may not translate to another.
- ☐ Grouping the most severely handicapped together may create the feeling of a "dumping ground" and lower staff morale.
- ☐ Mentally handicapped people (especially children and young adults) can best be provided with a range of learning experiences in mixed ability groups.
- ☐ Living and working environments should be as "normal" as possible and near enough to the family to maintain family and friendship contacts.
- ☐ Staff in small segregated units could become professionally isolated and introverted.

A good example are the special care units in ATCs/SECs being set up by social services as the hospitals run down. If staff and clients are not included in the full life of the centre then isolation and stagnation can set in.

Mental handicap and mental illness

With the present high prevalence of mental illness in the general population it would seem sensible for people wth a mental handicap to receive care from the general psychiatric services. There is, however, some uncertainty both as to how many mentally handicapped people also suffer from an additional mental disorder, and about the willingness of the general psychiatric service to take on this responsibility.

Surveys since 1967 have shown large variations in incidence, and while studies of hospital residents may record disorders created by institutional care, community care policies and their attendant stresses may cause an increase in neurotic conditions. A longer life expectancy among, for example those with Down's Syndrome, may bring a higher incidence of pre-senile dementia.

Kenneth Day in a MIND conference on "Care in the community" (MIND, 1983) argued that mentally handicapped people with a mental disorder have special needs which are not well catered for by general psychiatry.

The 1970 Census of Mentally Handicapped People in Hospital in England and Wales showed, not only quite a large number in psychiatric hospitals, but that while education and training was deficient in mental handicap hospitals, over 75 per cent of mentally handicapped persons in psychiatric hospitals received no education or training at all.

84

Table 9 *Prevalence studies of psychiatric disorder in mentally handicapped people*

Author(s)	Population studied	% psychiatric disorder
Leck *et al* (1967)	Hospital in-patients, all ages	37% all categories
Williams (1971)	Hospital in-patients, all ages	59% all categories
DHSS (1972)	Hospital in-patients, all ages	16% mild behaviour disorder 16% severe behaviour disorder
Forrest & Ogunremi (1974)	Hospital in-patients, adults	10% serious psychiatric disorder
Heaton Ward (1976)	Hospital in-patients, adults (review of surveys)	8–10% psychoses and neuroses combined
Ballinger & Reid (1977)	Hospital in-patients adults adult training centres	31% Significant psychiatric 13% disorder
Kushlick (1970)	Total population severely mentally handicapped	7% severe behaviour disorder
Corbett (1979)	Total population severely and mildly mentally handicapped adults, Camberwell	46% significant psychiatric disorder

(*from MIND*, 1983)

Without doubt integration in this area may require specialist provision in the short term and concurrent education and retraining to produce a generic service in the future.

Table 10 *Numbers of mentally handicapped people in residential units classified by diagnosis in the 1970 Census*

Mental Category	Type of hospital or unit				
	All		Mental Handicap	Mental Illness	Other and contractual beds
	Number	%	Number	Number	Number
All categories	64,173	100	57,837	5,1440	1,196
Severe Subnormality					
Alone	46,905	73	45,249	800	856
With mental illness	366	1	261	105	—
With psychopathic disorder	23	1	21	2	—
Subnormality					
Alone	15,067	23	11,793	2,935	339
With mental illness	1,622	3	348	1,273	1
With psychopathic disorder	190	1	165	25	—

Education

To ensure the consolidation of a service philosophy and delivery which is positive and affirming there will be a need both for resource allocation and public education (see McConkey and McCormack, 1983). If this happens then aspirations can become a reality:

"Disabled persons have the inherent right to respect for human dignity. Whatever the origin, nature and seriousness of their handicaps and disabilities, they have the same fundamental rights as their fellow-citizens of the same age, which implies first and foremost the right to enjoy a decent life as normal and full as possible" (from the United Nations Declaration of the Rights of Disabled People, 1975).

Reading

DHSS (1984), *Helping Mentally Handicapped People with Special Problems.*

BASW (1983), *Towards Extraordinary Services for People with a Mental Handicap.*

D. Norris (1982), *Day Care and Severe Handicap*, MENCAP.

J. Ryan and F. Thomas (1980), *The Politics of Mental Handicap*, Chapter 6: "Old Ideologies for New", Penguin.

C. Parker and J. Alcoe, "Finding the Right Way Out", *Social Work Today*, 16 April 1984.

M. Brock (1984), *Christopher: A Silent Life*, Bedford Square Press.

W. Wolfensberger (1972), *The Principle of Normalisation in Human Services*, Toronto.

MIND (1983), *Care in the Community: Keeping it Local.*

L. Ward (1982), *People First*, Kings Fund Project Paper No. 37.

R. McConkey and B. McCormack (1983), *Breaking Barriers: Educating People about Disability*, Souvenir Press

N. Carle (1984), *Key Concepts in Community-Based Services*, CMHP

M. Oswin (1984), *They Keep Going Away*, King's Fund Oxford University Press.

D. Felce *et al*, "Housing for Severely and Profoundly Mentally Handicapped Adults", *Hospital and Health Services Review*, July 1984.

D. Thomas (1982), *The Experience of Handicap*, Chapter 7, Methuen.

English National Board (1985), *Caring for People with Mental Handicap*, Section 2, ENB/Learning Materials Design.

E. Goffmann (1964), *Asylums*, Penguin.

10

Assessment and after

T he concept of assessment has over the years acquired a mystique which hides its clear dictionary meaning of an estimating or fixing an amount about something. Assessment in the broadest sense is something most people do all the time, estimating where they think they are in relation to certain goals and plotting further steps in their advancement. Certainly there are some tests that only pychologists are permitted to do, but that profession, far from hoarding a store of knowledge to itself, has been developing assessments that can be used by a wide number of people, including parents.

The first question relating to assessment is: What do we want to look at and what do we want that information to help us with?

Functions of assessment

To estimate the current position
- [ ] Social assessment of the individual within a family, or an evaluation of the living environment if in residential care.
- [ ] Baseline of behaviour and/or skills.

For service planning
- [ ] IQ classification, to ascertain how the individual compares with the average, eg an education department looking at future special education provision.
- [ ] Skills and adaptive/maladaptive behaviour, eg the HANC and HALO assessments developed by Shackleton-Bailey in Hampshire to ascertain the social services department's future requirements.

Prediction of future progress
- [ ] To draw up realistic individual programme plans (IPPs)

Profile analysis
- [ ] Looking at a large number of skill areas so that, deficits in one area (eg speech) can be improved with beneficial consequences to other areas.

Measurements of change
- [ ] Classification systems, from the 1913 Mental Deficiency Act's once-for-all certification to what Joanna Ryan has called "IQ fatalism", are of limited use if they are static in nature. Even the most handicapped person is likely to develop in very restricted areas and this should be charted, if for nothing else but to give the carers hope.

Assessment devices

A number of assessment forms have been devised over the past few years and these are some of the most well known:

Developmental tests
- [ ] Bayley Scales of Infant Development — for babies and young children.
- [ ] Griffiths Developmental Scale — for the young child.
- [ ] Behaviour Assessment Battery — advice for developing programmes for profoundly handicapped children.
- [ ] Portage — a home-based assessment and teaching method, with home visitors and parents working closely together.

Intelligence tests
- [ ] Stanford-Binet
- [ ] Wechsler Tests
- [ ] British Ability Scales

Tests for Skills and Adaptive Behaviour
- [ ] PAC — Progress Assessment Charts (Gunzberg).
- [ ] Copewell (Whelan and Speake).
- [ ] Vineland Social Maturity Scale (Doll).
- [ ] ELSI — Everyday Living Skills Inventory (Barker).
- [ ] Fairview Self-Help Scale.
- [ ] Pathways to Independence (Hester Adrian Centre).
- [ ] Adaptive Behaviour Scale (Philadelphia Centre).
- [ ] STAR — Social Training Achievement Record (Williams).

Assessment and training

Assessment should serve as a basis for future action, it is not an end in itself. Assessment of a person's skills and behaviour can give a baseline from which a programme can be instituted to achieve progress in certain areas.

People with a mental handicap often find difficulty in learning from experience and so any training programme needs to be carefully structured, imaginative, and arising from the motivation of the handicapped person and the most significant people to him — eg his parents.

The goals set need to be clear and realistically attainable so that everybody understands what is being aimed for and so that eventual success, however gradual, is certain.

There are now a number of excellent publications which help parents give their children the extra developmental stimulus needed, notably:

J. Carr (1980), *Helping Your Handicapped Child*, Penguin.
C. Cunningham and P. Sloper (1978), *Helping Your Handicapped Baby*, Souvenir Press.
R. Brinkworth and J. Collins, *Improving Babies with Down's Syndrome*, Down's Children Association.

Parents find the Portage scheme an invaluable aid because it gives them attainable goals to achieve even with profoundly handicapped children plus

Figure 27: *Alogorithm of the assessment/training process*

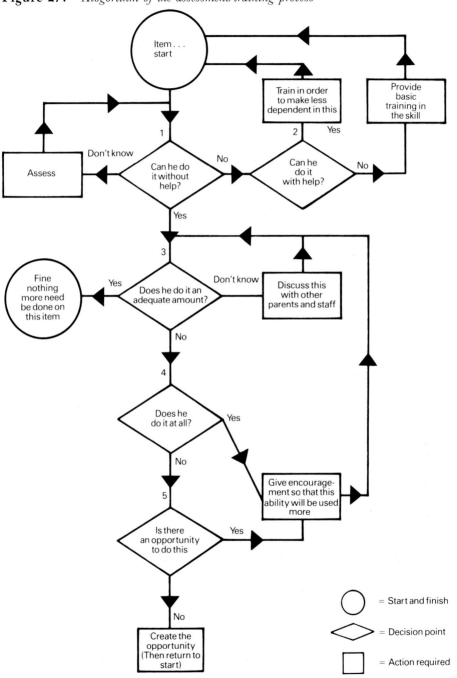

the encouragement of a home visitor.

For those coming up to school leaving age the Copewell system is being increasingly used because of its stress on everyday coping skills and the fact that, while it can be used by both parents and professional staff, the goals and achievements are readily understandable by the mentally handicapped person himself.

Copewell has four main areas of assessment which lead on to detailed training programmes:

- ☐ Self-help
- ☐ Social, academic
- ☐ Interpersonal
- ☐ Vocational

Crucially it pinpoints whether the opportunity exists for the individual to learn and carry out a skill, the lack of which opportunity often counts against a handicapped person, especially in hospital; and it looks at interpersonal coping which can make or mar the life-skills of anybody, handicapped or not.

Educational assessments

The 1981 Education Act and the attendant departmental circulars have incorporated assessment into the legislation so as to look at "the child as a whole person" and set out steps to meet his "special educational needs".

The Act lays a duty on education authorities to assess children who have a "learning difficulty" and gives parents the opportunity to request assessments within a framework where there is "... a partnership between teachers, other professionals and parents, in a joint endeavour to discover and understand the nature of the difficulties and needs of individual children" (Circular 1/83).

The Education (Special Educational Needs) Regulations 1983 lay down that the authority must take into account the parents' representations (regulation 8) and must seek educational, medical and psychological advice, and "any other advice which the authority considers desirable" (regulation 4).

Most authorities will request a social report from social services so as to ascertain any home circumstances which may bear on the child's educational needs. Good social work practice could lead to the social assessment being used to talk through the anxieties and expectations relating to the assessment and to using the pre-school leaving assessment to help children and their families look to the future (see figure 19).

Table 11 *Assessment procedures under the 1981 Education Act*

Summary of procedures
Children under two

Parent can ask for *assessment:*

District health authority must tell **parent**, then **education authority**, that child may have *special educational needs;*

Education authority may with *consent* of **parent**, and *must* at *request* of **parent**, make an *assessment*. It can be of any kind, and may result in a *statement of special educational needs* of any kind.

Children between 2 and 19

Authorities have a *duty* to *identify* children whose *special educational needs* call on the **authority** to *decide* on *special educational provision;*
Parents can request *assessment*, and **authorities** cannot *unreasonably refuse*.

Assessment

Notice to **parents** — *29 days* to comment;
If **authority** decides *not to assess*, must *notify* **parent**;
Parents must receive *notices* of any *examinations;* have right to be present and to submit information;
Parents who fail to see that their children turn up for examinations without *reasonable excuses* may be *guilty* of offence and *fined.*

After assessment

Authority may decide *not to make statement of special educational needs:* must inform **parent** of *right of appeal* to **Secretary of State**;
If **authority** decides to *make statement:*
   must serve *copy of draft statement* on **parent**;
If **parent** *disagrees* with any part;
   within 15 days can make *representations*, ask for *meeting* with **officer**;
   within further 15 days, ask for other *meetings* to discuss professional advice provided to authority (which must be given to parent as part of statement);
   within final 15 days from last meeting, make further representations to authority.
Authority, after considering parents' views can make *statement* in the same or changed form, or decide not to make it: *must inform* **parent**.
If *statement* is made, must be sent to **parent** with *notice of right to appeal*, and *name of person* to go to for advice and information;
Parent has *right of appeal* in writing to *local appeal committee*, which can *confirm statement*, or ask authority to *reconsider* it;
Parent has further *right of appeal* to **Secretary of State**.
Statements must be *reviewed* within every *12 months;*
Child with *statement must be re-assessed* between age of 12½ and 14½.
Authority *must see that special educational provision set out in statement is made.*

(from P. Newell (1983), ACE Special Education Handbook, *ACE)*

Behaviour therapy

Behaviour therapy is often thought of as a means of eradicating deviance but is much more relevantly linked to assessment and training. Many people with learning difficulties become trapped in a cycle of repetitious behaviour which can be very frustrating both for themselves and those caring for them. The teaching of additional skills can liberate them from dysfunctional methods of coping and enable them to progress.

Where behaviour problems do arise the therapist needs to look closely at the interaction, known as the ABC:

A	B	C
Antecedent	Behaviour	Consequence
Mother pays attention to another child	Tony wets himself	Mother smacks Tony

Clinical psychologists, who are likely to become involved from the CMHT in helping with such difficulties, no longer simply look at the behaviour in isolation but at the dynamics of the situation. Eradicating apparently deviant behaviour is no longer seen as enough in itself, as some self-destructive activities may be the handicapped person's only means of stimulation or gaining attention in a sterile environment.

The involvement of the subject, the selection of relevant coping skills, the instilling of confidence to use those skills, and the manipulation of the environment to create opportunities are the bases for assessment today.

Figure 28 *Summary of events and description of effects*

Consequating event	Known as	Effect on behaviour
Presentation of a reinforcer	Positive reinforcement	Strengthen
Presentation of a punishment	Punishment	Weaken
Cessation of reinforcement	Extinction	Weaken
Removal of punishing event	Negative reinforcement	Strengthen
Removal of reinforcing event	Response cost	Weaken

(*From C. Williams, 1980*)

Social workers should be receiving training in learning theory, help with developmental strategies being one of parents' prime needs, and getting involved with their clients in drawing up individual programme plans for future development.

Reading
C. Williams, "The Behavioural Approach", in G. Simon (ed) (1980), *Modern Management of Mental Handicap*, British Institute for Mental Handicap

W. Yule and J. Carr (1980), *Behaviour Modification for the Mentally Handicapped*, Croom Helm

C. Hallas *et al* (1982), *The Care and Training of the Mentally Handicapped*, Chapter 20 & Appendix 3, Wright-PSG.

11
Communication

As the latest report on mentally handicapped people with "special problems" states, "many mentally handicapped people have poorly developed language and communication skills" (DHSS, 1984). Hospital surveys have recorded figures such as 60 per cent of children and 18 per cent of adults having no speech at all, and though only the most profoundly handicapped children are likely to be admitted to hospital nowadays, a large proportion of pupils attending ESN(s) schools are likely to have recognised speech disorders, and/or developmental language delay.

Language development

Although developmental milestones are broad, normal child communication develops in well-defined progressive stages:

From 6 weeks to 6 months experiments making sounds for pleasure (babbling)
From 6 months to 9 months vocalises and gestures to gain attention
From 9 months to 12 months understands few familiar words like "no", and "bye, bye"; knows own name; shouts to attract attention.
12 months responds to own name; understands simple instructions if accompanied by gesture; often speaks first words
15 months says two to six recognisable words
18 months says six to 20 recognisable words
2 years uses 50 recognisable words; understands many more; begins to link words in two-word phrases
(*see M. Sheridan (1973)*, Children's Developmental Progress, NFER)

As in other learning development, mentally handicapped people require extra stimulation to acquire and maintain communication skills. Parents also can easily lose heart when their child does not respond to their talking. The task of the language therapist, therefore, is to provide both motivation, encouragement and positive programmes. Communication is a two-way process involving the person transmitting the message, and the person receiving it.

At one time the received wisdom was that alternative communication methods lessened the motivation to learn speech. Now it is recognised both that other methods can aid speech development and, that with the high incidence of speech disorders in this group (eg dysrhythmia, echolalia, tongue-thrust in Down's Syndrome etc — see glossary), other forms of communication are essential.

Alternative communication systems

- **Manual**
- ☐ *Sign Languages* (eg American Sign Language (ASL); British Sign Language (BSL)
- ☐ *Communication systems* (The Makaton Vocabulary; Paget-Gorman Sign System)
- ☐ *Signalling Systems* (Amerind)
- **Symbols**
- ☐ Blissymbolics
- ☐ Premack System
- ☐ Rebus Symbols

As indicated above, BSL is a language with all the complexity that this entails. The other manual and symbolic communication aids have various characteristics, for example Makaton, the most widely used, has a number of pros and cons in its use:

Table 12 *The Use of Makaton*

Advantages	Disadvantages
Widespread use (eg *circa* 95% of ESN(s) schools in 1982).	Some signs have an obscure derivation.
A complete language programme with a developmental sequence.	No direct correspondence with spoken English or BSL.
Relatively easy to learn, with language programmes available to to facilitate teaching.	Everyone in the environment(s) needs to learn the system.
Signs are relatively easy even for those with below average motor control.	

The 1984 DHSS report suggests that Makaton is the most useful of current systems where speech is very slow to emerge or seems unlikely to do so. It also says that Paget-Gorman will be useful to those whose comprehension of language is adequate but whose expression is marred by severely defective articulation. Lastly, the report believes that Bliss and other representational systems will help children with little or no speech and whose physical handicap makes manual signing impossible.

It is important that health, social services and education in any given area co-ordinate communication programmes so that the systems used are consistent in both living and work environments and when individuals move from one environment to another. At the heart of any language programme

Makaton vocabulary

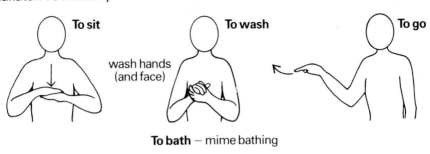

To sit

To wash — wash hands (and face)

To go

To bath — mime bathing

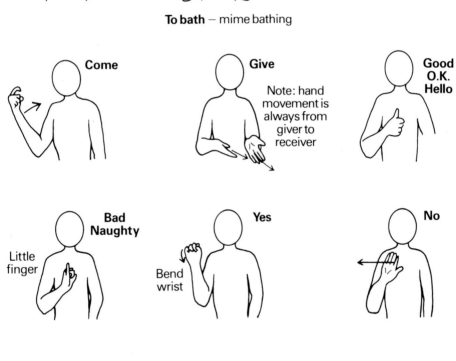

Come

Give — Note: hand movement is always from giver to receiver

Good O.K. Hello

Bad Naughty — Little finger

Yes — Bend wrist

No

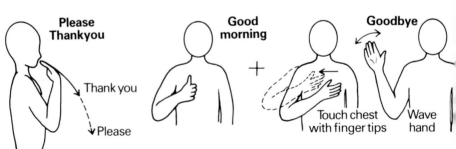

Please Thankyou — Thank you / Please

Good morning

+ Touch chest with finger tips

Goodbye — Wave hand

is the desire to communicate, and the basis of this is the commitment to form relationships. Language development will occur most rapidly when professionals relate to mentally handicapped people as people rather than do things for them or to them.

Assessments for communication

Some of the best known are:
- [ ] Reynell Developmental Language Scales (age range: 1½ to six years)
- [ ] Illinois Test of Psycholinguistic Abilities (age range: 2 to 10 years)
- [ ] Language Imitation Test (age range: ESN(s) school range)
- [ ] Peabody Picture Vocabulary Test (age range: 2½ to 18 years)

Reading
M. Walker, "Communication", in G. Simon (ed) (1980), *Modern Management of Mental Handicap*, MTP Press
DHSS (1984), *Helping Mentally Handicapped People with Special Problems*
C. Hallas *et al* (1982), *The Care and Training of the Mentally Handicapped*, Chapters 8 and 9, Wright-PSG.
Makaton Vocabulary Booklet is available from: The Makaton Vocabulary Development Project, 31, Firwood Drive, Camberley, Surrey

12
Financial provision

Judith Buckle's research for the Disablement Income Group reveals the extra costs of handicap for both individuals and families, and local surveys are constantly revealing the low take-up of benefit. Adequate finances can often enable families to surmount a crisis that might otherwise have laid them low. It is worth social workers having a close relationship with the local DHSS office who may themselves be taking active steps to promote the take-up of benefits.

The DHSS produces a leaflet setting out the benefits available for disabled people: *HB1 — Help for Handicapped People* (Benefit rates are likely to change every November and the amounts payable for each benefit are set out in the leaflet, *N1.196 — Social Security Benefit Rates*). There is also a leaflet on aids, *HB2 — Aids for the Disabled.*

Several voluntary agencies also publish information booklets:
The Disability Rights Handbook — published each year by the Disability Alliance, 25 Denmark Street, London WC2H 8NJ.
A-Z — published by Mencap.
After 16 — What Next?, published by the National Bureau for Handicapped Students, 40 Brunswick Square, London WC1N 1A2.

More and more local authorities are fulfilling their obligations to inform families of services under the 1970 Chronically Sick and Disabled Persons Act by producing information handbooks (eg *Coping with Mental Handicap in Crawley, Horsham and Mid-Sussex*, West Sussex County Council, 1985).

The provision of benefits is now so complex that anyone constantly working with disabled individuals and their families should have the current edition of *The Disability Rights Handbook*.

I have not attempted to duplicate the information set out in such a handbook, but the following *aide memoire* may prove useful:

Mobility benefits
Apart from Mobility Allowance other benefits are:
- ☐ *The Orange Badge Scheme* giving parking concessions to individuals or families with a permanent and substantial mobility problem. Available from social services.
- ☐ *Rail fare concessions*
- ☐ *Vehicle Tax Exemption* — if the person suffers from a permanent and

Table 13 *The main benefits for mentally handicapped people and their families*

Benefit	Claim from what age	Taxable	DHSS leaflet	Non-contributory	Means tested	Comments
Attendance Allowance	2 years	No	NI 205	Yes	No	Paid to the mentally handicapped person in two rates depending on the care he needs in terms of a) help with bodily functions b) supervision
Invalid Care Allowance	2 years	Yes	NI 212	Yes	Earnings limit	For women on their own caring for a handicapped person
Mobility Allowance	5 years	No	NI 211	Yes	No	Paid to an individual who is unable to walk or virtually unable to do so or where it would damage his health
Severe Disablement Allowance	16 years	No	NI 252	Yes	Therapeutic earnings limit	Can be claimed even if in continuing Special Education
Supplementary Benefit	16 years	No	SB 1	Yes	Limit on capital of £3,000	Can be claimed with SDA. Not affected by parent's means

substantial mobility problem and is in receipt of a) Attendance Allowance 2–5 years, b) Mobility Allowance 5 years plus.

☐ *Motobility*, a scheme to use the Mobility Allowance in order to lease a car.

Housing benefits

☐ *Housing Benefit* itself is mainly useful for those persons in group home accommodation or sheltered flats and not sponsored by social services.

☐ *Rate relief* — if additional facilities have been put into a house specifically to benefit a disabled person.

☐ *Adaptations* for council tenants can be done by the housing authority under Section 3 of the Chronically Sick and Disabled Persons Act 1970, while private householders may gain help from an amalgam of environmental health grants and additions from social services and voluntary funds.

Educational benefits

Education authorities should, under the 1944 Education Act, pay playgroup fees or provide a place in a nursery class in a special school from the age of 2 years.

Some education authorities pay an Education Maintenance Allowance to families on a low income when a child stays on at school after the age of 16.

Backdating claims

Though it is always best to claim at the right time, recent changes in the rules have meant it may be possible to backdate a claim if one can show "good cause" for this to be done. A person with a mental handicap, who cannot manage money for himself, is often accepted as automatically having "good cause" for a failure to claim benefit.

Appeals

Even apparently straightforward claims for benefits, eg a claim for Attendance Allowance in respect of a child at a school for children with severe learning difficulties, are refused alarmingly often. Claimants have the right to appeal, within a specified time — usually 28 days — against any decision taken by an adjudication officer or adjudicating medical practitioner.

It is vital to sort out whether a decision depends on what the law actually says, or whether it depends on a particular interpretation of the law, or on policy. There are some grey areas such as, in an application for Mobility Allowance, whether the degree of guidance a mentally handicapped person (without additional physical impairments) requires to walk between two given points constitutes his being "virtually unable to walk". This question has been the subject of a number of legal battles and the Disability Alliance issued a special "Checklist for Appeals on Mobility Allowance" in January 1985.

Most appeals go to a Social Security Appeal Tribunal but medical decisions in respect of Mobility Allowance, Attendance Allowance and Severe Disablement Allowance have a more complicated route (see *The Disability Rights Handbook* Section O).

In the case of appeals, organisations such as the Disability Alliance and Network for the Handicapped (see appendix 1 below) can give valuable assistance.

Dependent Relatives' Tax Allowance

Dependent relatives (from age 16) should be placed on the annual income tax form.

Away from home

If a mentally handicapped person enters residential care then his benefits are affected accordingly:

- ☐ Attendance Allowance stops after four weeks, though it can be claimed for days spent at home even if the individual is a long-term resident.
- ☐ Mobility Allowance is unaffected.
- ☐ Severe Disablement Allowance — individual only keeps the personal allowance.

Safeguarding the future

Parents whose dependant has a severe mental handicap worry about the future: who will look after their child's interests? Will he have enough money to live on, and, if they leave money in their wills, will this go to their child or be siphoned off by the state?

These questions are very complex and constantly affected by legislative changes. Mencap have, however, set up a special visiting service (Trustee Visitors Service), which operates after the parents' decease, and, under Gerald Sanctuary's direction, have investigated ways of protecting legacies.

Figure 29: *Protecting those left behind*

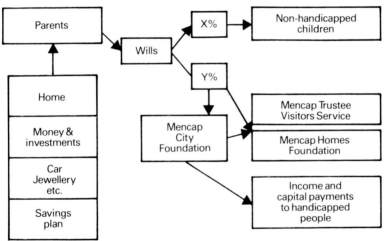

(*from G. Sanctuary (1984)*, After I'm Gone: What Will Happen to my Mentally Handicapped Child?, *Souvenir Press*)

Vaccine-Damage Payments

A scheme for paying a tax-free lump sum to compensate people who are disabled as a result of vaccination was introduced in 1979 (*DHSS Leaflet HB3*). There is a list of diseases against which a claimant must have been vaccinated and the vaccination must have been carried out in the UK after July 1948 (in the case of smallpox, before August 1971). The vaccination must also have been given when the claimant was under the age of 18 (except in the case of poliomyelitis and rubella vaccinations) or at the time of an epidemic.

Charitable funds

There are a variety of charitable funds but the one set up to help families with a handicapped child up to 16 years is:
The Family Fund,
Joseph Rowntree Memorial Trust,
PO Box 50,
York YO1 1UY.

Reading
N. Malin *et al* (1980), *Services for the Mentally Handicapped in Britain*, Croom Helm.
J. Stone and F. Taylor (1973), *Handbook for parents with a Handicapped Child*, Arrow.
R. Cohen and A. Rushton (1982), *Welfare Rights*, Heinemann Educational/*Community Care*.

Community Care publishes annually a wall chart on supplementary benefits each November in the issue coinciding with the November uprating. Copies may be purchased from *Community Care*, Sundry Sales, Quadrant House, The Quadrant, Sutton, Surrey SM1 4QQ.

13

The law and mental handicap

In the Mental Health Act 1959 mental subnormality and severe subnormality described the condition generally referred to as mental handicap. The definitions used were:

☐ *Severe subnormality*: "A state of arrested or incomplete development of mind which includes subnormality of intelligence and is of such a nature or degree that the patient is incapable of living an independent life or of guarding himself against serious exploitation, or will be so incapable when of an age to do so";

☐ *Subnormality*: "A state of arrested or incomplete development of mind (not amounting to severe subnormality) which includes subnormality of intelligence and is of a nature or degree which requires or is susceptible to medical treatment or other special care or training of the patient."

Almost all the Mental Health Act 1959 has been repealed by the Mental Health Act 1983, an Act which consolidated the law relating to mentally disordered persons. In the 1983 Act the new terms of mental impairment and severe mental impairment retain the concepts of (a) incomplete or arrested development, and (b) retardation of intelligence and a lack of social skills, but restrict the definition to those who are a danger to themselves or others.

☐ *Severe mental impairment*: "A state of arrested or incomplete development which includes severe impairment of intelligence and social functioning and is associated with abnormally aggressive or seriously irresponsible conduct on the part of the person concerned".

☐ *Mental impairment*: "A state of arrested or incomplete development of mind (not amounting to severe impairment) which includes significant impairment of intelligence and social functioning and is associated with abnormally aggressive or seriously irresponsible conduct on the part of the person concerned".

While mentally handicapped people will not be liable to detention under the Mental Health Act 1983, unless they display "abnormally aggressive and seriously irresponsible conduct" they remain eligible for services set out in health service and related legislation because of the broad definition of disability and vulnerability in the statutes.

Admissions to hospital and reception into guardianship

These provisions relate to anyone suffering from a mental disorder, defined in the Act as: "Mental illness, arrested or incomplete development of mind, psychopathic disorder and any other disorder or disability of mind".

This excludes promiscuity or other immoral conduct, sexual deviance or dependence upon alcohol or drugs.

There are compulsory admissions for assessment (section 2), treatment (section 3) and in an emergency (section 4).

Guardianship (section 7) may be used for mentally handicapped persons over the age of 16 years if that person is

☐ "suffering from mental disorder, being mental illness, severe mental impairment, psychopathic disorder or mental impairment and his mental disorder is of a nature or degree which warrants his reception into guardianship under this section" and if

☐ "It is necessary in the interests of the welfare of the patient or for the protection of other persons that the patient should be so received".

The essential powers of the order are to require the individual to live at a specified place; to attend for occupation, training or medical treatment; and to see a doctor, social worker or other designated person.

For detailed information see R. Brown (1983), *The Approved Social Worker's Guide to the Mental Health Act 1983*, Community Care/Business Press International

Child care

Although the health service legislation empowers local authorities to provide substitute and respite care to families with handicapped children, this does not negate the duty of social services departments to safeguard the interests and welfare of the child himself through the use of the child care legislation if necessary.

All substitute and relief care provision should be carefully monitored to ensure that the child's interests are not being subordinated to the needs of parents. Section 9 of the 1959 Mental Health Act, still extant, makes it clear that nothing in any enactment prevents a local authority from receiving into its care under Section 2 of the Child Care Act 1980, a child who is mentally handicapped. The interests of children in specialist hospitals and schools should be considered from a child care viewpoint.

Education

Since the Education (Handicapped Children) Act 1970 was implemented in 1971, severely mentally handicapped children can no longer be classified as unsuitable for education at school.

The 1981 Education Act (implemented in 1983) replaced the former system of classifying children, based on categories of handicap, with the concept of children with "special educational needs". These pupils should be educated in ordinary schools subject to consideration of the parents' views; the ability of the school to meet the special needs; the efficient education of other children; and the resources available.

While a number of children may need special educational provision, assessments are now a formal process involving both parents and other agencies. A joint DES and DHSS circular (LAC (83) (2)) stressed the need for co-operation with social services.

As in the case of child care law, mentally handicapped children in hospital should not be exempt from mainstream provision. Section 56 of the 1981 Education Act does allow the LEA to provide education elsewhere than in a school, but only in "extraordinary circumstances".

Housing

The Housing Act 1957 requires local housing departments to consider the needs of their area and to prepare schemes for providing housing to meet those needs. They are empowered under the Act, and under the Housing Act 1974 to provide a range of accommodation which would be suitable for mentally handicapped people, including single dwellings and bed-sitters.

Section 2 of the Housing (Homeless Persons) Act 1977 imposes a duty on housing departments to provide accommodation for mentally handicapped people (among others) if they are homeless or threatened with homelessness. Admission to hospital for the social reason of lack of accommodation should not occur.

The right to vote

For some years informal patients in hospitals could vote if they had a home address. Now changes brought about through the Mental Health Act 1983 and the Representation of the People Act 1983, mean that residents in mental handicap hospitals, who are not mentally disordered, and who are in hospital only because they have no home, can use the hospital as a place of residence for voting purposes.

Hospital managers are bound to give informal patients information as to their rights, and the individual must make a declaration without assistance, ie he must understand the activity that he is taking part in.

Marriage

Mentally handicapped people have, in the main, the same rights to marry as every other citizen, provided none of the usual impediments apply. The marriage could be void, however, if either party did not give valid consent because of "unsoundness of mind" (Matrimonial Causes Act 1973, section 12 (c)); or if at the time of the marriage either party was suffering (whether continuously or intermittently) from mental disorder within the meaning of the Mental Health Act, this being "of such a kind or to such an extent as to be unfitted for marriage" (Matrimonial Causes Act 73 S 12 (d)).

Protection of property

Should a mentally handicapped person be admitted to a hospital or other accommodation and it appears that loss or damage may occur to his movable property then, under section 48 of the National Assistance Act (NAA 48) the local authority has a duty to take reasonable steps to prevent this loss or damage.

Police procedure

Social workers should note that police officers detaining a mentally handicapped person should be guided by the Home Office circular to chief constables (109/76) which states that the interview should be in the presence of a third party, parent "or other person in whose care, custody or control he is, or of some person who is not a police officer (for example a social worker)". Documents arising from the interview should also be signed by the third party.

SOCIAL SERVICES FUNCTIONS

Legislation can be divided into mandatory (ie laying a duty on the authority to provide a service) and permissive (ie, enabling the authority to provide that service should it wish to do so). Legislation in the mental handicap field is mainly permissive, which has resulted in at best an uneven and at worst an undeveloped service (Roberts, 1978).

Ascertainment and information

Section 29 of the National Assistance Act 1948 (NAA 48) states that local authorities have the power to make arrangements for promoting the welfare of persons who are blind, deaf and dumb, and other persons who are substantially handicapped by illness, injury or congenital deformity.

Section 1 of the 1970 Chronically Sick and Disabled Persons Act (CSDP 70) lays upon the local authority the duty to inform itself of the number of persons within their area to whom Section 29 of the NAA 48 applies.

Section 1 (2) (a) and (b) further states that every local authority should publish information concerning services; and ensure that someone who uses a service is informed of other services which may be "relevant to his needs".

DHSS circular No 45/71 goes further in saying that disabled people should be encouraged to come forward to "facilitate the gradual building up of comprehensive lists of people needing help".

Supportive services

As stated above, the local authority has the power to promote the welfare of disabled people (section 29, NAA 48) or make arrangements for a voluntary organisation to do so on its behalf (section 30, NAA 48).

In DHSS circular LAC 19/74 the Secretary of State directs local authorities to provide "social work and related services to help in the identification, diagnosis, assessment and social treatment of mental disorders and to provide social work support and other domiciliary and care services to people living in their homes and elsewhere".

Section 21 of the National Health Service Act 1977 (NHSA 77), in conjunction with schedule 8, makes it a duty of local authorities to make arrangements to prevent illness, and for the care and after-care of persons suffering from such illness.

Paragraph 3 (1) of schedule 8 lays a duty "to provide on such a scale as is adequate for the needs of their area. . . home help for households where such help is required owing to the presence of a person. . . handicapped as a result of having suffered from an illness or by congenital deformity''.

Section 2 (1) of the CSDPA 70 empowers social services departments to provide practical assistance in the home, recreational facilities, help in travelling to facilities, advice and assistance with aids and adaptations, the facilitating of holidays, the provision of meals and the provision of a telephone.

Social work support for mentally impaired persons will be affected by the appointment of ''approved social workers'' under section 114 of the Mental Health Act 1983.

Day care

Section 29 of the NAA 48 empowered authorities to provide day centres and now section 21, in conjunction with schedule 8 of the NHSA 77, makes it a duty of local authorities to make ''provision for persons whose care is undertaken with a view to preventing them from becoming ill, persons suffering from illness and persons who have been so suffering, of centres or other facilities for training them or keeping them suitably occupied and the equipment and maintenance of such centres'' (paragraph 2 (1) (b)).

Since the 1944 Disabled Persons (Employment) Act the Department of Employment has had a duty to assist disabled people find work through training and rehabilitation schemes. The 1944 Act has been largely repealed by the Employment and Training Act 1973, which placed training and rehabilitation schemes under the employment service and training service agencies.

Residential care

Section 21 of the NAA 48 places a duty on the local authority to provide ''residential accommodation for persons who by reason of age, infirmity or any other circumstances are in need of care and attention which is not otherwise available to them''.

The authority is also to have regard to the fact that varying needs will require different accommodation. DHSS circular No LAC 19/74 also directs authorities to provide '' . . . residential accommodation (including residential homes, hostels, group homes, minimum support facilities) or other appropriate accommodation''.

The NHSA 77 is now the most relevant statute in its power to authorities to assist in care and after-care through the provision of residential accommodation — section 21, 2 (1) (a), or ancillary or supplementary services such as holidays. This replaces section 12 of the Health Service and Public Health Act 1968 (HSPHA 68).

Section 44 of the HSPHA 68 extended section 26 of the NAA 48 to give power to authorities to provide residential accommodation for disabled people in premises provided by voluntary organisations (including housing associations).

Co-operation

Section 22 (1) of the NHSA 77 states that "in exercising their respective functions, health authorities and local authorities shall co-operate with one another in order to secure and advance the health and welfare of the people of England and Wales".

Reading

L.O. Gostin (1979) "The Law in England the Wales", in M. Craft (ed), *Tredgold's Mental Retardation*, Bailliere Tindall

L.O. Gostin (1983), *A Practical Guide to Mental Health Law*, MIND

G. Roberts (1978), *Essential Law for Social Workers*, Oyez

P. Newell (1983), *ACE Special Education Handbook*, Advisory Centre for Education

Encyclopaedia of Social Services Law and Practice, Sweet and Maxwell

R. Brown (1983), *The Approved Social Worker's Guide to the Mental Health Act 1983, Community Care*/Business Press International

14
Medication

S ince about a third of all mentally handicapped people suffer from epilepsy and a number will show signs of psychotic behaviour, a basic knowledge of drugs and their side effects is necessary. New drugs are constantly coming onto the market and unsatisfactory products being withdrawn by the DHSS, so no static list is satisfactory.

Up-to-date details are set out in the current editions of *Mims*, published monthly by Haymarket Publishing Ltd, Medical Division, Regent House, 54/62 Regent Street, London W1A 4YJ; and *The National Formulary*, published by the BMA, Tavistock Square, London WC1H PJP

Psychotropic drugs can be divided into:

☐ Anti-depressants
  ○ Primarily mood-elevating (Tricyclics)
  ○ Disinhibiting monoamine oxidase inhibitors (MAOIs)
  ○ Stabilising (eg Lithium)
  ○ Newer drugs
☐ Major tranquillizers which are antipsychotic drugs, being non-hypnotic sedatives.
☐ Minor tranquillizers which lack antipsychotic effect and with a calming, hypnotic action.
☐ Anticonvulsants for control of epilepsy.

Most of the drugs in these groupings have side-effects. It is most important that it is ensured that the client and parents know what these are. Major tranquillizers should be used for *as short a time as possible*, as drugs such as Melleril have Parkinsonian side-effects. Even a minor tranquillizer like Valium causes physical withdrawal in up to 50 per cent of cases as well as the inevitable psychological withdrawal.

One of the main additional problems with any medication is its interaction with other prescribed drugs. Some handicapped people may be on several drugs for, say, cardiac problems and epilepsy. If an anti-depressant is then added, the combinations of possible maleffects rise considerably. If the client is on several drugs then he is likely to need blood tests to check the serum levels. Likewise anybody with epilepsy should have the chance of a regular consultation with a neurologist.

Table 14 *Some drugs in common use for mentally handicapped people*

Drug	Trade name	Indications	Side effects
Tricyclics			*Similar for all Tricyclics*
Amitriptyline	Tryptizol	Depression	Can cause 1) Epileptic fits and cardiovascular toxicity 2) Dry mouth, blurred vision, constipation, drowsiness, urinary retention 3) Should not be given within 14 days of an MAOI
Imipramine	Tofranil	Depression. As an adjunct to treatment for enuresis	
Doxepin	Sinequan	Depression	Less risk of cardiovascular toxicity
Trimipramine	Surmontil	Depression	
Dothiepin	Prothiaden	Depression	Less likely to trigger epilepsy
MAOIs			
Tranylcypromine	Parnate	Depression	All MAOI drugs may cause a sudden rise in blood pressure when taken with certain other drugs eg Tricyclics, tranquillizers and food containing tyramine (eg cheese, bovril, pickled herrings, bananas, animal livers, broad beans etc) Dry mouth, agitation, nausea and headache are also common.
Phenelzine	Nardil	Depression	

Lithium compounds

Generic name	Brand name	Use	Side effects
Lithium Carbonate	Priadel	Manic states and to prevent mood swings in affective psychoses	For all Lithium compounds regular blood tests should be taken to assess the serum level. Vomiting, ataxia, drowsiness
Baclofen	Lioresal	For spasticity. May reduce self-mutilation	Confusion and drowsiness
Newer drugs — Tetracyclics			
Mianserin	Noral	Depression and anxiety	Fewer side effects than Tricyclics
Major tranquilizers			
Chlorpromazine	Largactil	Disturbed and psychotic behaviour or extreme agitation	Drowsiness, depression, Parkinsonism, dry mouth
Thioridazine	Melleril	Psychotic disorders	Drowsiness and dry mouth. Lower toxicity and side effects than Largactil
Haloperidol	Serenace	Psychoses and also neuroses with depressive features	Parkinsonism, so usually used in conjunction with an anti-Parkinsonian drug such as Kemadrin
Trifluoperazine	Stelazine	Disturbed and psychotic behaviour	Restlessness
Flupenthixol decanoate	Modicate	Maintenance treatment for psychotic disorders eg Chronic Schizophrenia	Parkinsonian effects and depression
Fluphenazine decanoate	Clopixol	as above	Less Parkinsonian effect
Benperidol	Anquil	Control of deviant and anti-social sexual behaviour	Parkinsonian effect

Drug	Trade name	Indications	Side effects
Minor Tranquillizers			
Diazepam	Valium	To relieve anxiety and tension in the absence of psychosis, or intravenously or rectally for status epilepticus	Drowsiness and constipation, avoid alcohol
Chlordiazepoxide	Librium	Anxiety and tension	as above
Lorazepam	Ativan	Anxiety and tension	as above
Anticonvulsants			
Ethosuximide	Zarontin	Petit mal	Drowsiness, depression, nausea, anaemia, ataxia
Sodium Valproate	Epilim	All types of epilepsy	Gastric irritation
Phenytoin	Epanutin	Grand mal and focal epilepsy	Short term: nausea, weight loss, headache long term: blood disorders and ataxia
Carbamazepine	Tegretol	Grand mal and focal epilepsy	Not to be combined with MAOI therapy
Primidone	Mysoline	Grand mal and focal epilepsy	Nausea
Clonazepam	Rivotril	All types of epilepsy	Drowsiness
Phenobarbitone	Luminal	Grand mal and focal epilepsy	Headaches, nausea, hyperkinetic behaviour

Reading

C. Hallas *et al* (1982), *The Care and Training of the Mentally Handicapped*, Chapter 16, Wright-PSG

J. Bicknell, "The Use of Medication", in M. Craft, J. Bicknell and S. Hollins (eds) (1985), *Mental Handicap: A Multidisciplinary Approach*, Baillière Tindall.

G. Simon (ed) (1981), *Local Services for Mentally Handicapped People*. Chapter VII, British Institute of Mental Handicap.

Appendix 1
Useful names and addresses

Macaulay Road, London SW4 0QP Tel: 01720 8055

National Autistic Society, 276, Willesden Lane, London NW2 5RB
Tel: 01 451 3844

National Association for Deaf Blind and Rubella Handicapped Children,
311, Grays Inn Road, London WC1X 8PT Tel: 01 278 1000

Royal National Institute for the Deaf, 105, Gower Street, London WC1E
6AH Tel: 01 387 8033

Spastics Society, 12, Park Crescent, London W1N 4BQ
Tel: 636 5020

Spina Bifida and Hydrocephalus Association, Tavistock House North,
Tavistock Square, London WC1H 9HJ Tel: 01 388 1382

NB For a full list of support groups see *Useful Addresses for Parents with a
Handicapped Child* available from Mrs. A. Worthington, 10, Norman
Road, Sale, Cheshire M33 3DF

Voluntary Resources

Camphill Village Trust, Delrow House, Hilfield Lane, Aldenham,
Watford WD2 8DJ Tel: Radlett 6006

Care Concern, Ruthin, Clwyd, North Wales. Tel: 08242 4343

Christian Concern for the Mentally Handicapped, 171, Oxford Road,
Reading, Berkshire RG1 7U2 Tel: Reading 587800

Cottage and Rural Enterprises (CARE), 9a, Weir road, Kibworth,
Leicester LE8 0LQ Tel: Kibworth 3225

Home Farm Trust, 57, Queen's Square, Bristol BS1 4LF
Tel. 0272 23746

L'Arche Homes, 14, London Road, Beccles, Suffolk Tel: 0502 715329

United Response, 1, Thorpe Close, Portobello Green, London W10
Tel: 01 960 5666

N.B. MENCAP publishes a list of residential homes in England and
Wales; while Care Search is a computerised register of a variety of care
situations which aims to match need and resources. It is run by United
Response. Tel: 01 980 5666

Finance

DHSS Attendance Allowance — Norcross, Blackpool FY5 3TA
Tel: 0253 856123

DHSS Mobility Allowance — Norcross, Blackpool FY5 3TA
Tel: 0253 52311

DHSS Vaccine-Damage Payments Unit, Norcross, Blackpool FY5 3TA
Tel: 0253 52323

Disability Alliance, 25, Denmark Street, London WC2 8NJ
Tel: 01 240 0806

Disablement Income Group, Attlee House, Toynbee Hall, 28,
Commercial Street, London E1 6LR Tel: 01 247 2128

The Family Fund, PO Box 50, York YO1 1VY Tel: 0904 21115

Legal

Court of Protection, 49, Chancery Lane, London WC2A 1JR
  Tel: 01 405 764
MENCAP Legal Section, Golden Lane, London EC17 0RT
  Tel: 01 253 9433
Network for the Handicapped, 17, Princeton Street, London WC1R 4BB
  Tel: 01 831 8031 or 01 831 7740

Organisations for professionals

Association of Professions for the Mentally Handicapped, 126, Albert St.,
  London NW1 7NF Tel: 01 267 6111
Association of Residential Communities for the Retarded (ARC)
  PO Box 4, Lydney, Glos. Tel: 0594 530398

Research centres

Department of the Psychiatry of Mental Handicap, St. George's
  Hospital, Cranmer Terrace, London SW17 0RE Tel: 01 672 1255
Hester Adrian Research Centre for the Study of Learning Process in the
  Mentally Handicapped, The University of Manchester M13 9PL
  Tel: 061 273 3333
Kings Fund Centre, 126, Albert Street, London NW1 7NF
  Tel: 01 267 6111
National Centre for Down's Syndrome, 9, Westbourne Road, Egbaston,
  Birmingham B15 5TN Tel: 021 454 3126
The Wolfson Centre, Mecklenburgh Square, London WC1
  Tel: 01 837 7618

Alternative family care

British Agencies for Adoption and Fostering (BAAF), 11 Southwark
  Street, London SE1 1RQ Tel: 01 407 8800
Parents for Children, 222, Camden High Street, London NW1 8QR
  Tel: 01 485 7526/7548

Information

Dial UK, 117, High Street, Clay Cross, Derbyshire Tel: 0246 864498
Help for Health, South Academic Block, Southampton General Hospital,
  Southampton SO9 4X7 Tel: 0703 777222 Ext. 3753
In Touch (Mrs A. Worthington), 10, Norman Road, Sale, Cheshire M33
  3DF Tel: 061 962 4441
National Association of Citizens Advice Bureaux, 110, Drury Lane,
  London WC23 5SW Tel: 01 836 9231

Support groups (general)

Contact-A-Family, 16, Strutton Ground, Victoria, London SW1P ZHP

Tel: 01 222 2695
Kith and Kids, 6, Grosvenor Road, Muswell Hill, London N10
  Tel: 01 883 8762

Personal relations

Sexual and Personal Problems of the Disabled (SPOD), 286, Camden
  Road, London N7 0BJ Tel: 01 607 8851

Aids

British Red Cross Society, 9, Grosvenor Square, London SW1
  Tel: 01 730 0672
Disabled Living Foundation, 346, Kensington High Street, London W14
  8NS Tel: 01 602 2491
Equipment for the Disabled, Mary Marlborough Lodge, Nuffield
  Orthopaedic Centre, Headington, Oxford OXY 7LD Tel: 0865 750103
Muscular Dystrophy Group of Great Britain (see "Organisations and
  support groups for specific conditions", above): *With a Little Help*
  booklets on aids and adaptations.

Education

Advisory Centre for Education (ACE) 18, Victoria Park Square, London
  E2 9PB Tel: 01 980 4596

Periodicals

Communications, Newsletter, Parents Voice, MENCAP, 117–123, Golden
Lane, London EC17 0RT
Current Awareness Service, Mental Handicap, Mental Handicap Bulletin, BIMH,
  Wolverhampton Road, Kidderminster, Worcestershire DY10 3PP
In Touch, 10, Norman Road, Sale, Cheshire M33 3DF

Leisure and holidays

National Federation of Gateway Clubs, 117–123, Golden Lane, London
  EC17 0RT
The Disabled Sports Foundation, 10, Little Turnstile, Holborn, London
  WC1V 7DX
Toy Libraries Association, Seabrook House, Wyllyotts Manor, Docker
  Lane, Potters Bar, Herts. EN6 2HC Tel: 0707 44571

NB MENCAP publishes a holiday information booklet each year, and
the Voluntary Council for Handicapped Children (see "General
organisations", above) publishes fact sheets on holidays and leisure
pursuits.

Appendix 2
Supporting services/benefits check list

NAME: Date of birth:
Registered as handicapped   Yes/No

	Informed	Details
Financial		
Attendance Allowance		
Mobility allowance		
Severe Disablement Allowance		
Invalid Care Allowance		
Family Income Supplement		
Supplementary Benefit		
Free school meals		
Free milk		
Play School fees		
(Social services)		
(Education)		
Rent/rate rebate		
House improvement grant		
House adaptation grant		
Telephone		
Voluntary sources		
Family Fund		
Miscellaneous		

Practical

Aids/equipment adaptations

Sector aids	(Indoor)
	(Outdoor)
DHSS	(Indoor)
	(Outdoor)

Disabled driver/passenger badge

Home help

Family aide

Family care worker

Day care/child minding

Voluntary worker

Residential care —	Short term
	Long term

Housing

Fostering/link family

Holiday

Other

Social

Voluntary associations

Parents group

Voluntary visitor

Clubs — eg PHAB, Gateway club

Introduction to

other parents

other handicapped person

Day centre

Occupational therapy

Education

Toy library

Play school

Nursery school

Liaison with education department:
           Ordinary school

               Special school

               Educational psychologist

               Peripatetic teacher

Transport

Health/medical

Physiotherapy

Speech therapist

Psychiatric support

Child guidance

Nursing aids(dressings)

(Incopad roll, special pants, etc.)

Community Mental Handicap Team

Other

Training/employment

Training centre

College

Rehabilitation course

Sheltered workshop

Job centre (DRO)

Employment

Appendix 3
Changes in terminology

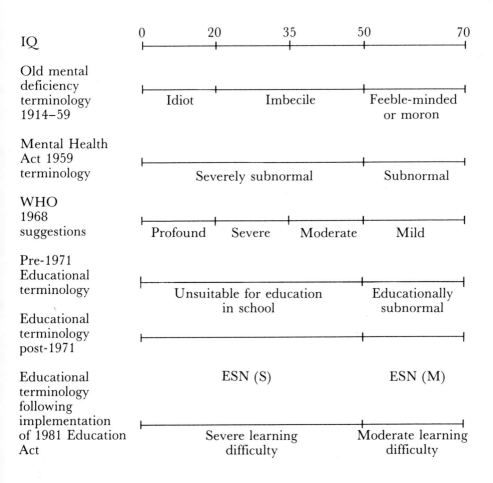

IQ	0	20	35	50	70

Old mental deficiency terminology 1914–59: Idiot | Imbecile | Feeble-minded or moron

Mental Health Act 1959 terminology: Severely subnormal | Subnormal

WHO 1968 suggestions: Profound | Severe | Moderate | Mild

Pre-1971 Educational terminology: Unsuitable for education in school | Educationally subnormal

Educational terminology post-1971

Educational terminology following implementation of 1981 Education Act: ESN (S) | ESN (M) / Severe learning difficulty | Moderate learning difficulty

Appendix 4

Legislation and reports particularly relevant to the mental handicap service

Date	Report	Legislation	Comments
1913		Mental Deficiency Act	Created four categories: ☐ Idiots ☐ Imbeciles ☐ Feeble-minded ☐ Moral Defectives Obliged local authorities to ascertain the number of "defectives" in their area. Statutory supervision of "ascertained defectives".
1914		Elementary Education (Defective and Epileptic Children) Act	Obliged local authorities to provide special schools for those children who are "dull and backward" but not "imbeciles".
1927		Mental Deficiency Act	Widened the definition of mental handicap and added the training and occupation of "defectives" to the duties of local authorities.
1939	Departmental Committee on the Voluntary Mental Health Services (Feversham report)		Favoured an all-purpose mental health social worker who would provide: ☐ supervision of early cases of mental and functional disorder. ☐ after-care of mental hospital patients. ☐ statutory and voluntary supervision of "mental defectives". ☐ follow-up of children presenting problems of behaviour.

Date	Report	Legislation	Comments
1946	Report of Care of Children Committee. (Curtis report).		Mentally handicapped children seen as a medical responsibility and recommended provision apart from other children.
1946		National Health Service Act (implemented in 1948)	Transfer of mental handicap institutions from the local authority to the NHS. Creation of a unified mental health service.
1957	Royal commission on Mental Illness and Mental Deficiency.		
1959	Report of the Committee on the Welfare of Children in Hospital (Platt committee).		Stressed the importance of catering for children's emotional needs in the hospital setting.
1959		Mental Health Act	Introduced new terminology: "subnormality" and "severe subnormality". Allowed social services authorities to accommodate mentally disordered people in residential care. Created mental welfare officer to carry out supportive and statutory functions.
1959	Report of the Working Party on Social Workers in the Local Authority, Health and Welfare Services (Younghusband report).		Recommended improved training and a better career structure for social workers in the mental health setting.
1968		Health Service and Public Health Act.	Provisions for local authority services (amended by the NHS Act, 1977).
1969	Report of the Committee of Enquiry into Allegations of Ill-Treatment of Patients		Revealed both specific instances of cruelty and general failings of the hospital system.

Date	Report	Legislation	Comments
	and Other Irregularities at the Ely Hospital, Cardiff.		Published in the same year as Pauline Morris's study of mental handicap hospitals, *Put Away*.
1970		Chronically Sick and Disabled Persons Act	Laid a duty on local authorities to inform themselves of the numbers of disabled people who might need their services, and in turn inform them of the services available.
			Some of the specific provisions in the Act have never been properly implemented by some authorities because the CSDPA 1970 was a private members bill and therefore no money was made available to the local authorities by central government.
1970		Local Authority Social Services Act (implemented 1971)	Created generic social services departments out of the children's mental health and welfare departments (based on the Seebohm report of 1968).
1970		Education (Handicapped children) Act (implented on 1 January 1971)	Brought severely mentally handicapped children into the education system, who had previously been classed as "ineducable".
1971	*Better Services for the Mentally Handicapped —* DHSS White Paper.		Laid down recommen dations over the whole range of services and set target dates for the implementation of a move from hospital to "community care".
1972	Report of the Committee on Nursing (Briggs report).		Recommended changes in the training of nurses.
1974	Social Work Support for		

Date	Report	Legislation	Comments
	the Health Service (Otton report).		
1974	Butler committee on mentally abnormal offenders.		Recommended regional secure units
1974	Report of the Committee of Enquiry into South Ockenden Hospital.		Revealed ill-treatment of patients, overcrowding and poor levels of care.
1975		Children Act	Enshrined "the welfare principle" in law and gave an impetus towards looking at children in hospital in the same way as other children in residential care.
1976		Education Act	Looked towards the 1981 Act in its recommendations for integration.
1976	Report of the Committee on Child Health Services (Court report).		Stressed the need for handicapped children to be treated as children first.
			Proposed an integrated child health service with district handicap teams serving the needs of families.
1976	National Development Group, Pamphlet One, *Mental Handicap: Planning Together*		The NDG pamphlets set guidelines for service development and urged multi-disciplinary co-operation both in planning and in service delivery (e.g. setting up community mental handicap teams).
1977	Normansfield Hospital Enquiry report		Revealed a repressive hierarchical regime deleterious to the well being of residents
1977	NDG Pamphlet Two, *Mentally Handicapped Children: A Plan for Action.*		

| --- | --- | --- | --- |
	Pamphlet Three, *Helping Mentally Handicapped School Leavers.*		
	Pamphlet Four, *Short-Term Care for Mentally Handicapped People: Suggestions for Action.*		
	Pamphlet Five, *Day Services for Mentally Handicapped Adults.*		
1978	NDG, *Helping Mentally Handicapped People in hospitals.*		Argues for a social work service in mental handicap hospital.
1978	Report of the Committee of Enquiry into the Education of Handicapped Children and Young People (Warnock report).		Recommended the abolition of the categorisation of handicapped children and is the forerunner of the 1981 Education Act in its proposals.
1979	Report of the Committee of Enquiry into Mental Handicap Nursing and Care (Jay report)		Proposed a unified training for nursing and social services staff, but looked beyond this to propose a local model of care with a move away from segregated services
1980	*Mental Handicap: Progress, Problems and Priorities.*		Evaluated progress since the 1971 White Paper.
1981	*Care in Action: A Handbook of Policies and Priorities for Health and Social Services in England.*		Put forward the essential elements in a locally based service.
1981		Education Act (Implemented 1983)	Abolished the categorisation system. Pupils with special educational needs are, in principle, to be educated in normal schools, contingent on certain considerations. Assessments are to be carried out at certain ages and in partnership with parents (see chapter 10).

Date	Report	Legislation	Comments
1982	All Wales Strategy for the Development of Services for Mentally Handicapped People.		
1983 (Jan)	*Helping to get Mentally Handicapped Children out of Hospital* (DA (83) (2))		
1983 (March)	*Care in the Community* (Green Paper)		Made a number of proposals concerning financial arrangements to speed community care.
1983		Mental Health Act	New categories of "mental impairment" and "severe mental impairment". Removes most mentally handicapped people from mental health legislation (See chapter 13).
1984 (Feb)	*Helping Mentally Handicapped People with Special Needs.*		Report on services needed for those with additional sensory disabilities and behavioural disorders, and elderly people with mental handicap.
1985 (Jan)	*Community Care: With Special Reference to Adult Mentally Ill and Mentally Handicapped People*		House of Commons Social Services Select Committee warned of the dangers of an inadequately funded community care programme.

Appendix 5
Glossary of terms

Actiology — the study of causes of disease and disorder

Anoxia — oxygen deficiency in organs and tissues and the disturbance resulting therefrom

Ataxia — failure to co-ordinate the actions of the various muscles involved in performing movements

Athetosis — uncontrolled movement of limbs, often associated with cerebral palsy

Cephalic — of, or relating to, the head

Diagnosis — the art and science of identifying a disease, a prerequisite to treatment

Dysrhythmia — stuttering

EEG — (electroencephalogram) — a brain wave tracing made to help in the diagnosis of epilepsy etc.

Echolalia — repeating the utterance, or part of it, of the person attempting to communicate

Epilepsy — a nervous disorder of varying severity, marked by recurring explosive discharges of electrical activity in the brain. *Petit mal* — a fit characterised by a loss of consciousness, usually so fleeting that it is unnoticeable. *Grand mal* — a fit usually associated with falling, violent threshing of limbs and the emptying of the bladder, followed by sleep. *Status epilepticus* — a series of grand mal attacks following immediately after one another which may endanger the life of the person unless medication is administered intravenously. *Focal epilepsy* — another form of seizure due to an abnormal discharge from a specific area in the brain and characterised by abnormal behaviour. *Pyknolepsy* — extremely frequent petit mal attacks

Hemiplegia — paralysis of one side of the body (Quadriplegia — paralysis of both arms and legs. Paraplegia — paralysis of the legs only)

Mental disorder — mental impairment etc — see chapter 13

Spastic paralysis — rigidity of muscles — eg in cerebral palsy

CMHT form devised by the Mid Downs CMHT

Minutes of the community mental handicap team   /   /19   *Part 1*

Name and Address	DOB	Diagnosis	Referred by	Reason for referral	Action required by keyworker allocated	Additional Comments

Present:

Apologies

Additional Distribution

Part 11:- *Feedback on cases referred in previous meetings (see also individual evaluation forms)*

/   /19

Name	Progress so far	Keyworker (confirmed/changed)	Further action

Part 111	Policy matters		Action